Hairy Vaj, Please...

My Journey on OkCupid

Reenie Raschke

Illustrations by Alice Raschke

Hairy Vaj, Please...
My Journey on OkCupid

Reenie Raschke

Illustrations by Alice Raschke

Sidekick Press
Bellingham, Washington

Published 2021
Printed in the United States of America
ISBN: 978-1-7363538-1-3 (hardcover) | 978-1-7365358-2-0 (paperback)
LCCN: 2021906230

Sidekick Press
2950 Newmarket Street, Suite 101-329
Bellingham, Washington 98226
sidekickpress.com

Reenie Raschke, 1962-
Hairy Vaj, Please: My Journey on OkCupid

Illustrations by Alice Rashke
Cover design by Creekside Collaborative

Dedication

For Alice~
Thou art thy mother's glass

Follow your light

Reenie ♡

x

Alice

Foreword

Here *lies the body of a captain.*
Foundered in the waves, collected by the sirens.
Oh, wise women of the sun—Oh what have we done?
Save this frail one lost by Poseidon.
—Deb Talan

Loss is a useful muse for story, implying nothing ahead but gain. The bravery required to dive into a new, uncharted future brings light to the ridiculous, and grants permission to gargantuan discovery.

This is the story of a single girl, in truth, a grown woman in her fifties without a lick of sense on her journey to understand love, attachment, and her home therein.

The changing roles and practices of man and woman make for a slippery slope on the pathway of this middle-aged *jeune fille*. One can indeed find a cornucopia of allies in this world, yet locating the stationary partner seems elusive—no doubt as a result of my own transgressions.

I am a voyeur by trade. I use a glass lens to make permanent the portrayal of human expressions. As a photographer, I find it much easier to document others' joy and attachments than I do my own. I can detect, in watching a lover's trusting glance, security and longevity. I make art of the feelings I observe in my clients, my people. Yet, in my personal life, I fear love is illusory. Or, is it?

I yearn for connection with a troubling hunger. The joyful flow of a dance entitled "we" keeps my search alive. To achieve it, I would need to fearlessly open up to painful truths and wobble on board my leaky ship equipped with only a tattered suitcase-heart. With thin skin devoid of protection, I could and would get hurt.

No soul worthwhile, I would determine, is exempt from injury. So af-fected are we all by the relationships that weave our sometimes colorful, sometimes burdensome shawl.

I would learn many parables illustrating the oddity and humanity of our men and women, consider mistakes and misunderstandings forged along the way.

My task to find love would be the work for which all of my prior work was merely preparation. Following an ever-present circle of light, the trip was just too piquant to pass over.

It is the process, my dear, not the product.
—Louellyn Post, my mother

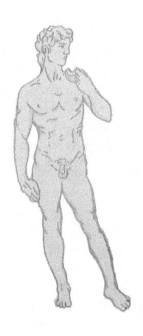

When in Rome

When I found months of texts between my lover, Mike, and "Kate Mortgage Broker," shortly after we'd made love in our cozy rented bed west of the Tiber River in Rome, I assumed that our five-year relationship was tragically over.

This had been my first trip abroad. I had waited a lifetime. As a teen, Mother had invited me several times to travel with her, yet I was always too busy with my all-encompassing social life. Now, at fifty-four, my dream was coming true with my twenty-five-year-old daughter, Alice, and her bohemian Zimbabwean boyfriend, Tinashe. We had smoothly traversed through Amsterdam, Bruges, the French countryside, Paris, and Marseille. After several weeks living out of a suitcase, we three met up with Mike in Northern Italy's Lake Como.

Mike and I had been living together for half a decade. He'd wanted to show us the fairy-tale Italy he had enjoyed in his youth and had seemed enthusiastic to do so. I don't know if he was hoping, during our trip, that I would not find out about this affair back at home in the San Francisco Bay Area, or hoping that I would. While he slept late that autumn morning in our Trastevere Airbnb, I unplugged his phone to use the charger, when a message flashed across the screen. Viewing the text, I froze.

> Have you told her? God I
> love you so much.

I'd met my Scoundrel, Mike, at a local watering hole back in Oakland, California, where many of our villagers loiter and consort on warm summer nights. Having recently published a photo essay of my woodland village, I was dropping off a copy of my book entitled, *My Town Montclair*, for the bartender, Joe.

"Watch this, this guy won't serve me."

To my left sat a darling boy, or was he a man? He accorded me the familiar pleasure of running into a friend from a high school math class. He inserted himself into my personal space with a wry smile.

"Of course he will," I reproached, "he's in my book. What would you like? I'll get it for you."

Making himself comfortable on the stool beside me, this gentle new fellow thumbed through my book. What a darling character, I thought, as I watched his black eyes scan corner-to-corner on each photograph. He had an inordinate amount of neat, short hair, so black it was nearly blue, and I wondered if perhaps he'd dyed it. Not particularly tall, he appeared unthreatening and playful. I felt the call to hold his hand like I would a child's.

Joe set a vodka-cranberry on a napkin in front of me, rolling his eyes in warning. This bartender had been protecting me from predatory men for years, and was skilled at guiding my instincts when mine weren't sharp.

"My name is Mike." His eyes swept over me, landing on my *décolletage*. "Why don't I know you? How long have you lived in Montclair?"

"Thirty years." I turned my knees toward him. "I raised my kids here."

Mike went on to explain that he was born in this town and had also raised kids the same ages as mine. It seemed impossible that we'd not crossed paths once in all these years living parallel lives in a small community.

"I live up here." I pointed to the hill above the bar. "My kids went to Montclair Elementary."

"*Ah*, we're on the other side," he said. "But still, you'd think we'd have met at some soccer or baseball event with the kids."

Glancing back, he nodded to a young woman sitting alone at a table not twenty feet from where we were seated. She was clearly perturbed.

"Oh, I gotta go. I'm on a date."

We speedily exchanged contact information as he dismounted his bar stool, like a child sliding down a railing. What a strange little man.

The following morning, I found a text from Mike.

> I think you're super hot and would like to see you again if you're not married.

> I am.

> Ok, well, I'd like to see you again anyway. We can be friends. I'd like you to meet my dog.

His text was then followed by a cell phone picture of a goofy Bernese Mountain Dog, tongue hanging down to his collar.

I acknowledged his image with an image of my own dog, an Australian Shepherd, tricolored, similar in size and color to his own.

> OMG! I'll meet you at the Redwood Amphitheatre in twenty minutes!!!

> Alright

With a deep sigh, I closed my laptop and the Photoshop project I'd been working on. A new friend could certainly be of benefit. My marriage was disintegrating, and the loneliness was tearing me apart. And that was how it began.

As we walked the Redwood trails together he shared his love of the same deep woods I'd been calling my playground for decades. Somehow, I'd not noticed the carvings in the rocks at the highest point of the Oakland Hills summit.

"Look, here's a carving dated 1870! These people were horse-drawn, coming up to picnic a hundred years ago," he explained, delighting my curiosity.

Our bookend dogs romped beside us wherever we went. He always had a plan for our next adventure.

"I want you to come to Thirsty Thursday and meet all of my friends from kindergarten."

As the months flew by, my kids launched into college, settling in their dorm rooms, selecting new friends far from home. My second husband, Paul, had lost his job and was losing his grip on reality and our marriage. By spring, I knew the marriage was over. Mike helped me look for possible live/work situations in downtown Oakland should I lose the house in the portending divorce. One afternoon, after viewing a ramshackle abandoned cookie factory on the corner of Crack and Prostitute, he pronounced, "No girlfriend of mine is going to live in the ghetto. You're living with me. Let's rent your house out until you find a better solution."

"Girlfriend" was a new word. I liked the sound of it, as well as the possible relief it offered.

"Let's," short for "let us," felt auspicious. We broke the seal and rolled from friendship into lovers.

Five years flew by living with Mike in his Starship-Enterprise-view house perched on the precipice of Oakland Hills. It needed a woman's touch, and I felt qualified. I wanted everything to reflect him. Emulating the fall-colored leaves I would gather on the trail, combined with the WPA brown log cabins with their Tyrolean red lettering, I displayed my whimsical, growing love for him. Creating color palettes from Wes Anderson's film, *Moonrise Kingdom*, and focusing on his lifetime on that Redwood-lined hill, I was in full artist's mode. I loved to find unusual watercolors of the woods in galleries and garage sales, old skis, Kodachrome images of his childhood to fill his house with crafts and moody colors. I relished building an outdoor shower and dog-washing station with river rock alongside a shoddy mason and lunatic plumber I had hired. The house, cantilevered over the San Francisco Bay, was divine, yet, over the course of those five years, I often felt we were placeholding our hearts in anticipation of the big quake that would wipe this whole fiasco off the map.

Mike, or "Scoundrel," as he was aptly named as a child, was endearing and acted as though he was immortal. His constant effervescence convinced people that he was.

It was not unusual to find texts from other women on his phone. He met women everywhere: in bars, waiting in line for a hot dog, on a transit train, at musical venues. His charisma was contagious and easy. His sporty demeanor put folks at ease.

"That's the nicest person I've ever met!" he often said after exchanging phone numbers with an Uber driver.

Because these exchanges were often made hastily—on a ski lift chair or in a loud restaurant—he usually obtained just a first name. To keep them straight, he attached identifiers to these contacts, such as Hot Diane, Cami Stewardess, or Edgy Kristy. Once, while we were driving to the mountains for a ski trip in a blizzard, an incoming text on his phone from Wendy Hardware Store illuminated.

I want to suck your dick.

"That's just a joke we play," he'd whimpered when I stopped breathing.

This, and other inappropriate behaviors, were simply a part of the package that I found exasperatingly adorable. This demeanor resting somewhere between Dick Clark, Peter Pan, and Jeff Spicoli was the sum of my Scoundrel who liked to ride Big Wheels down the steep Oakland trails and skateboard through town. It was easy to know where he was as his car windows were always down; Tom Petty, Tower of Power, or AC/DC blaring his arrival, an icy vodka-cran sloshing in his cup holder.

The reason for his ever-juvenile behavior at fifty-eight was explained to me in *The Big Fish Story* that everyone seemed to know. When Mike was nine and staying at his father's hotel in Mexico, the locals extolled the virtues of the fabled Golden Fish that was impossible to catch.

This elusive dorado had forever taunted the villagers, and it was proclaimed that should anyone secure this mighty Mahi, they would win a life of luck. Naturally, Mike caught the fish, and was granted good fortune for the remainder of his life.

In 1972, the Mexican government seized his father's hotel, but the luck of the Scoundrel would endure. It had to be more than luck, though, that provided this strong net.

I'd wondered aloud about the large-sum checks that landed in his mailbox every month. Apparently, after years as an insurance broker, his father opted to buy a large plot of land in the once uninhabited California midcoast town of Paso Robles. Now, the prime acreage was home to a significantly profitable mobile home park. Literally running itself, this assurance of a stable income, in tandem with the luck of the Golden Fish, enabled Mike to live less cautiously than the rest of us.

My life with him had been a Bonnie-and-Clyde-style adventure, and the famous last ride for this Miss Parker was inevitable. Everybody knew we were wrong for each other, but they let it flow because the two of us were just so damn fun together. We had tickets to every coveted rock concert on the calendar. We played Scrabble at the country club and hot-tubbed every evening. He knew all the shortcuts to supporting our haphazard exploitations, and taking the day off to hit the beach and find oysters was a common event.

Now, in Rome, that this latest discovery of Kate Mortgage Broker was revealed, I let Alice and Tinashe know, while they zipped up their travel backpacks with camera gear and water bottles, that I would not be joining them to visit the Vatican that morning. Rather, I took my lover's phone and the keys to our room and opted to seek out the Spanish Steps. I wanted to postpone the pain as long as I could, and, in complete emotional disarray, getting lost seemed the wisest thing to do.

I dizzily bumped through the crowded alleys following various screenshots of maps on my phone. One can't rely on a moving blue orb without Wi-Fi, and this kind of blurry lack of direction was soothing, as it gave me a project to work out, like a treasure map.

After an eternity, I found the steps I'd sought and they were, as I'd hoped, cinematically enormous. As big as Rome, as big as God, as big as music, as big as love, yet still not as big as my breaking heart as I scrolled through months of clandestine conversations.

Who was this girl and how did she know my Scoundrel so well?

> When I put little one
> down to bed, she said to
> me, Mommy I wish Mike
> could stay here.

So, there was a youngster involved. This could not be good.

As I started to unpack the details of the last six months of our relationship, I had recalled Mike being significantly more irritable and impatient. His Jackie Gleason fits of rage had caused friends to confide that he simply was not treating me well enough.

It had been a successful year for me. The photography studio I ran had several strong months, including the wedding and family sessions of some celebrity basketball players. Photography is a very unstable means of work; one never knows how each month will deliver, yet I'd landed some destination gigs. Thus, I was on the road more than usual.

I'd been blindly excited about the planning of this European trip and spent countless hours sleuthing out and organizing planes, trains, and lodging.

Alice and Tinashe, fresh out of college, had taken over the basement of Mike's house, and, upon our return, Scoundrel had promised them free lodging with us for a year. How would that pan out if our relationship were to implode?

"I love you" was so easy for Mike to say because he loved everything. He loved beaches, he loved skiing, he loved sex, he loved strangers and adventures, he loved being generous like a child sharing his collection of shiny Tonka trucks. He marveled over the most absurd things like manhole covers and squirrel feces, making them all seem fascinating. When a siren rolled by, he would jump in his car and follow the fire truck, announcing, "I'm going to help them!" Which he frequently did.

I found an old videotape of Mike collecting a medal of honor from the mayor of Oakland for his assistance in the great Oakland Hills fire. With a garden hose in one hand and a Coors Light in the other, he had single-handedly saved several homes.

"The garbage man is coming!" he'd squeal, throwing down the morning paper. Running out the front door, he'd flail his arms to the early toiling men, "Thanks, dude!"

"Listen to this!" he announced, beaming one evening at the local pub, sweat pouring down his forehead. "A UPS truck was overturned on the side of the road. I got out to help, and while I was holding the driver, he died in my hands!"

His stories were incredible, yet always turned out to be true. As if living on another plane, he dove with vibrant zest into life. Bizarre circumstances seemed to orbit him.

Still, as dazzling as he was, and as nice as this tall gal looked on his arm, the truth was that he didn't really love me. Never had I heard the word "forever." His embrace never felt fully assured. Plans pretty much covered the next month, and though my constant life goal had been to find the man who would care for me with enough security to allow me to wear a sun hat and sandals for the rest of my life, this was not the man. For the past several months, he had hinted at how I could move out. I knew this was coming. I'd been ignoring the truth.

I examined the dates of these text conversations, trying to determine how this had slipped by me. While I had been in Los Angeles, he and the Mortgage Broker had been in Big Sur. While I had attended Alice's college graduation, they had been at the Big Game. He was moving on to the next adventure—without me.

After I had tortured myself to my limit, soaking in every last excruciating word of those texts, I lifted myself from the alabaster steps at the base of the spewing fountain and stared up at the church. A young girl was cooling her hands in the fountain spray next to me. The place was packed with tourists and swirling children playing chase, oblivious to my veiled pain. I slipped Mike's phone in my pocket, feeling both hurt and shameful for digging into my lover's heart.

"Perhaps he loves this girl," I thought.

I took my time returning to the room where we were staying. Turning into an alley, I stopped into a shop displaying the big blue "T" for Tibacchi—Italian for tobacco. Scoundrel despised cigarettes and always cursed me when I smoked them.

"Good," I thought. "What will he do? Leave me for a mortgage broker?"

When in Rome.

We hit three more romantic destinations in Italy, sparing no expense on boat rides through colorful hillside villages, dining in exotic restaurants, and buying unforgettable clothing and soaps that one can only collect in Italy.

Of course, we argued. He was sorry that he had betrayed me and lied for so many months. "It just happened" was his reasoning, which, I have to say, is about as honest as he could be.

He said that this was a gal introduced to him by what I'd thought was a mutual friend. "She needs me," he explained over a grilled cheese sandwich in Cinque Terre.

Did I not?

We decided to make the best of the remainder of the trip and jumped off high cliffs, swam and paddled through azure waters, made love daily, and drank expensive wine on terraces. It was as if we'd received the edict that I would be dead in two weeks and we were making the best of our last days together.

Kate Mortgage Broker continued to text and phone, imploring that he catch the next plane home. I could hear her voice demanding that he be exclusive, which, after Old Napoli, he conceded to.

This love between us, or whatever it had been for all of these years, was over, and I had a lot to think about. How had he moved from exclusive with me to exclusive with her without me even knowing it? How could she ask such a thing from a guy who was living with someone? That someone, being me.

I meditated on why he was still making love to me. Was this a last *hoorah*? I was wracked with pain. I felt numb and helplessness, mixed with resistance, denial, resolve, and unrest.

The unaccountable thing was that I did not feel angry. Mike was not the type of guy to really share his feelings beyond what was fun, but he seemed in this situation to show a glimmer of substance, even if it wasn't toward me. Months prior, he should have sat me down to explain that things were not working for him, that he genuinely felt a shift in his plans, but finding that day was impossible for him. Waiting for something to happen is often worse than having it actually come down with a sudden thud. I was dizzily weary and woozy there at the finish line.

When planning this trip six months prior, all four of us had booked our flights separately. Alice and Tinashe were to split with us at this point and do the English countryside to visit Tinashe's relatives. Mike had been, needless to say, eager to get home to be close to a woman that as far as I knew wore the surname Mortgage Broker.

I had, six months prior, opted for the affordable WOW airlines. Affordable, as it offered far fewer direct connections, with layovers. Why not explore Ireland alone and stay for a week? Given my formal first name is Noreen (though I have no Irish blood) and the fact that Mike seemed encouraging at the time, Ireland had been my choice.

"You should totally take another week by yourself," he had said those months before. "You'll love Ireland!"

Now that I had the news of Ms. Mortgage Broker, I understood why he'd been so emboldened. I felt troubled letting Mike out of my sight, yet what good would come of going home with him and witnessing this collapse?

Mike had chosen the lodging for our last night in Naples, and it was obvious that he was no longer trying to impress me. Rather than a charming Airbnb, he'd booked a tiny hotel room in the loudest part of the city, close to his escape, the airport in Naples.

The room was dingy and small, with a faint smell of other people's clothing. I normally would sit down to research the best restaurant for an evening odyssey, but it was late, we were deflated, and the thought of sitting face-to-face with my Scoundrel for the last time was underwhelming. We opted for the hotel cafeteria, where the pasta was obviously boxed, a far cry from what we'd been experiencing.

I was starving, yet not hungry. The wine was bitter, as if from a bottle that had been open for two weeks. I should have sent it back, but we'd ordered at a cash register, and the pasty-faced kid who had rung us up didn't strike me as a master sommelier.

I drank it all in one swill that initially pinched my face, then coaxed me into the familiar dull relief from truth. Exhaling slowly, in hopes of avoiding the bends as I ascended from this surreal territory, I let my plastic fork fall on the table, wishing, at least, it had been flatware for effect.

"Don't do this, baby," I cried, searching his eyes for his heart.

"I don't know what's gonna happen, Reen." Mike looked exhausted. His face, tanned from several weeks of vacation, looked wan and hungover.

Pretending that all of this did not happen would have been an easier choice for both of us. What if we just didn't go home?

I was sick with grief all night, sobbing and clutching onto Mike's resistant body in bed. We used to hold hands while we slept. Now, on the eve of the end, I reached for his hand and was met with a limp, grasp-less paw, numb to my besiege.

Attempting Mother's solution for discomfort, I closed my eyes and examined my pain, giving it a shape and color that I could breathe into. This practice, meant to target, dissect, and manifest a path for healing, often worked with indigestion and injuries. Mom could get you down a freezing ski slope with a broken leg or ferry you to the prom with a zit the size of a cherry with her powers of suggestion.

Find it, find it, find it. I closed my eyes hard in the darkness. I was met with an inky, deep-blue, spiraling abyss, with no solid place to focus. No starry light to guide me, just a chasm of undoing.

I was unloved. I had no place to occupy.

The following morning, we flagged a cab to the airport, and while I visited the restroom, we lost each other for twenty minutes. When at last Scoundrel emerged from a kiosk, he was irrationally angry.

"Where have you been?! Why are you such an idiot?" Mike lunged at me, his jaw clenched and eyes ablaze with indignant fury. His dark hair fluffed up like a rooster about to crow.

The levity of his Hawaiian shirt with little topless hula girls on it felt out of place. Observers in the crowded airport slowed and looked at me as if to ask, "Are you safe? Do I need to interfere?"

Barely as tall as I was, in khaki cargo shorts exposing his slender calves tucked into bulbous white tennis shoes, people often found us an odd couple. He was too short to be in charge of me. When he barked like this, though, people noticed.

"Mike, it's inappropriate to speak to a human like that," I whispered.

His alarming fulmination, visibly mounting over time, made a great deal of sense to me once I'd learned of his change of heart. Like a teenager needing to launch, the only way to make the break was with a fight, and he could pick one now over a lost glove. I had neither the strength nor the will to engage him. I knew whose arms he was wanting, and I had no choice but to succumb.

I looked into his eyes and saw the boy I had loved. There was no doubt that I knew him deeply, and I knew he meant me no harm. That was clearly why he hadn't told me. He liked me and I liked him. It had been impossible for either one of us to choose the day I would leave his house, but friends had warned me, and everybody knew.

I walked him to the edge of his TSA check-in and held him for what felt like an hour. His scent was not his usual Old Spicy smell of adventure;

he'd not even shaved that morning. His aroma was earthy and profoundly honest. I took him in with one last, long, slow breath, then turned toward my terminal.

Heaving my far-too-large purple suitcase onto the scale, I boarded the big purple jet, greeted the purple flight attendants, settled my cell phone into my purple purse, and secured my seatbelt. What was it with this purple theme? Before I'd left for this grand tour, I, for some reason, thought the color would set me apart from other tourists, but apparently I was behind the marketing curve of WOW airlines' branding.

I felt like such a rookie with this inexperienced equipment and poor choices. I'd been on the lam for two months and used half of what I'd packed in this stupid TJ Maxx eyesore. Had I really thought that I would wear a black sleeveless romper or a red evening gown that I'd packed to impress someone? Dragging the ridiculous Violet Beauregarde over cobblestones and wrestling it up five floors of fourteenth-century quarters had been absurd. Alice had been abroad for three months and had been just fine with a third of my booty, wearing the same threadbare suede jacket and cut-off shorts every day.

"It's all just bullshit," I reprimanded myself. "You are a weak-ass loser, Reenie. When are you going to get strong and take some control of your fucking, lame-ass life?"

The thud was clear and resounding; it was time I find myself, all by my big self.

Luck of the Irish

Behind me now were the tall, solid bicyclists I'd encountered in the canals of Amsterdam, the lush and fecund flora and folk of the French country-side, and the theatrical, fiery singers of Italy with faces of marble. Gone was my comical man-boy and his socially conspicuous exploits. I was now on the brink of Dublin and her foreboding weather, Shetland ponies, and leprechauns.

My swimsuit was now deep in my suitcase, my sweater and journal in my carry-on where the camera always remained at the ready. Like any new place, the first day in Dublin was odd. Being alone amplified my vulnera-bility.

Nothing worked in Ireland and it smelled like cabbage. The air was mossy yet urban. I couldn't find my Airbnb that was supposed to be a quick walk from the airport bus. My electrical adapter was wrong and finding an open shop in the south end that might sell the part was more work than I had the fortitude for. My loneliness was crippling, direction, impossible. So, after settling in, I found the nearest pub for dinner.

The Rose and Thistle that bragged the best meat pie in Dublin seemed a worthy choice. The first women I encountered almost immediately at the barley-scented bar were Rose and Mary. I found their classic Irish names a poetically charming coincidence. Pouring my heart out, I spent the entire evening extolling my last two tragic months to my captive audience of two yummy new chums of my gender.

"Well, lamb," Rose admonished in her glorious Celtic brogue, "you'd be knowin' all along it was fool's gold, now didn't ye?"

"Well, of course," I whimpered.

"I think what you will be needin' now is some good medicinal music."

She lifted her heavy arm, exposing an endearing set of dimples where an elbow might be, and pointed out toward the center of the Temple Bar neighborhood.

"Go to the music, darlin', there, to O'Donoghue's."

"Oh, fer sure," Mary chimed in, nodding her head, eyes agape.

Mapping out directions to the prescribed location, I snapped a screenshot on my cell phone and gathered my belongings.

"I appreciate you." I looked deeply into Rose's eyes and then into Mary's.

As I walked through the colorful cobblestone avenues, I thought about Mary's hand-knit sweater and wished I had photographed these women. Something about them felt affirming, as if they were put in place, like a street sign, especially for me.

O'Donoghue's was classic Dublin. The dim alehouse was lined with drunken boys singing what felt like a familiar camp song. Sensing my naivete, one offered to buy me a pint of Guinness.

"I don't really care for beer," I said, recalling the watered-down Coors Light that Scoundrel and his buddies swilled. "How about a glass of wine?"

He grimaced at me as the bartender put a larger-than-American-sized glass of whiskey in front of me instead.

"There's your wine, lass."

The malty spirit burned my lips and tongue as it ushered my confusing grief down my throat and into my stomach with an audible splash.

"Perfect. Thank you," I said. "Apparently, I am here for my medicine. A woman named Rose told me this was the place for music."

"Give her another." The boy winked at me. "I've a prescription to fill."

I watched this stormy, dark-haired man-child move from his tall stool to a corner of the dark bar. There, an alcove of benches made a semicircle, a grotto. Picking up his *bodhrán* drum, he gave it a few strokes, as if to call his clan. He must have been at least twenty-one to be in the bar, well, maybe not, but he was most assuredly too young for me.

"Geez," I thought, giving my head a jarring shake. "Is this what's gonna happen? Are you going to be looking for a new lover? You're not ready, girl."

Like a call to action, a circle formed around the handsome boy—a guitar, fiddle, and what seemed a simple mouth pipe. They started with a fierce war song, drowning me with guilt. How concerned could one be about a broken heart when there had been barefoot battalions dying from the cold?

God, that must have been horrible.

I listened carefully to the classic stories that carried me back to childhood songs. Legendary dramas of beguiling dark-eyed lassies and sons leaving mothers for war.

Then came the perfect emotional massage, clearly the elixir Rose and Mary had foreseen. The age-old folk song, *The Water is Wide*, was one I could sing. I'd known it forever.

I leaned my back against an oak, thinking it was a mighty tree;
But first it bent and then it broke. So did my love prove false to me.

These feelings were not my invention. The savory comfort was all-consuming, and because it was dark, obscure, and far from home, I could cry, so there I did, most gratefully.

An elderly man with a golden scruff of a beard approached me and set his giant, gentle hand on my knee. "What's troubling you, girl?"

It was lifting to be called "girl." At fifty-plus, I was hardly a child, but his soft eyes had a patriarchal assurance that caused me to draw near.

"Some asshole." I wrung yesterday's mascara from my eyes and managed an exhausted smile.

Hoisting his glass high above the crowded tavern, he shouted, "Some asshole!"

To which every arm in the bar rose and every voice responded in chorus, "Some asshole!"

"And what did he do?" another interloper called out.

"He shit the bed," I said with a sigh.

"He shit the bed!" the ensemble roared back.

"Well then, fuck 'im!" This time a woman's voice led the throng.

"Well then, fuck 'im!"

Night after night, I returned to O'Donoghue's for additional wallops of inspirational adrenaline. By day, I toured the cliffs I longed to jump from and swore I would not attempt to phone home, knowing full well what was happening there.

I paced a lot, wringing my hands, longing for some magic to take the pain of this untethered fear away. Like holding my breath under water, I had to endure the pain and patiently wait for relief. Cigarettes were some comfort, as I hadn't been allowed them in Scoundrel's company. Nobody was berating me. I just had to stay alive.

Finally, slowly, a strong power came over me that felt very much like God or chocolate syrup. An instinct, an afflatus that said, "Let go. I've got it from here. Just stay here and open your heart."

This strange assuredness began on a weird bus tour through the craggy green- and rust-colored countryside, of which there is no shortage in Ireland.

This tour had promised to show us a fine and mystical adventure of interesting attractions, but after four hours, the unfamiliar tourists and I were doing little more than silently watching the lunar landscape spin by. I wondered what my traveling colleagues were processing, and if anyone else was feeling inescapably sad.

Each in their own private daze, perhaps the slender blonde was thinking of work or food, maybe the heavy-set gentleman with the clear "W" in his brow was enduring his arthritis. The student from Germany conceivably knew more about the geology of this landscape and was delighted with his enlightened outlook. The irritable couple sitting adjacent to me should have divorced many years ago, their lack of polite exchange an indication.

Usually, I like to sidle up to strangers and learn from their stories, yet this day, it was a struggle just to keep breathing. As we traversed over endless glen and dale, I listened to the *bump-bump-shoosh* of our wheels and breathed my anthem to the rhythm, *my breaking heart, shhhh, my breaking heart, shhhh.*

After what felt like forever, a four-year-old and his mum stood up and staggered their way to the front of the cab, the little one clutching her leg.

"My child needs a loo," she pleaded.

Why on earth this woman thought a full-day tour had been appropriate for a young child was beyond me. We had been sitting still for hours and I hadn't heard a sound from him. To Europe's credit, I had been noticing on my trek many resilient children strengthened further by trying circumstances.

We pulled over to a handcrafted slag wall in the wilderness. I felt the poor child's humiliation as forty tourists watched to see if he could do it. As he stood at the wall, his mother clumsily unbuttoned his trousers, patiently enduring his complaints.

Then, by some classic Celtic augury, an old toothless man entered the left of our vision, leaning upon another cinematic stone wall. Like a leprechaun that instantly popped onto the scene, I half expected to see a rainbow arcing into a papier-mâché pot of gold beside him. We passengers incredulously searched one another's faces, eyes blinking in mutual amazement, as we'd not previously noticed his surreal stone house across the road.

He was a gnomish old fellow, and as he tottered toward the boy, he waved his craggy arm. "Come, lad," he said, as he motioned toward his wife, a stocky, female version of himself, who emerged from the low, curved door under the thatched roof. The boy and his mother graciously entered the house, bowing low to make the clearing. It was fucking magic, like animation.

"You've got to document this," my heart beckoned, as I grabbed my camera bag. I jumped up and skittered out of the bus, ignoring the driver's protests.

Approaching gently, in fear that he might disappear like a timid doe, I smiled at the old man, who was even better close-up. His weathered hands seemed to indicate that he had built this wall, and several others without assistance. His eyes were cloudy-yet-expressive, and when he smiled, exposing only gums, the misty afternoon opened with gossamer light. I must have been twice his height.

"This is awfully nice of you," I started. "I have my camera here with me. May I photograph you?"

He positioned himself in front of his little fairy house, and, puffing up his chest, displayed his best gummy smile.

"Are you married?" he sputtered.

"Well, that is a very long story, my friend, but no, I am not."

"I wonder how many single ladies are on that bus of yours?"

I pulled out my camera.

I have been pulling out my camera to make sense of this life for many decades. At seventeen, Mom and Dad gave me the photographic coffee-table book, *The Family of Man*, as a birthday gift. The gorgeous collection of verse and prose alongside spellbinding black-and-white images of humans doing human things led me first to my room to emote, then out to shoot with one of Dad's cast-off film cameras.

In my teenage bedroom, belly down on my brass bed, I pored over depictions of love, pain, joy, and trial. When I finished, tears streaming, I started over again, yearning to prolong the arousing drug of art.

"Thou art thy Mother's glass," Shakespeare explained, "and thee in she calls back the lovely April of her prime."

"Yes," cooed my heart. "Do it again. I'm on to something here."

As I turned the pages, time froze.

"Look harder, look deeper, learn what you see," something in me insisted. "All are needed by each one; nothing is fair or good alone."

The words of Emerson, Bible verses, and song came into brilliant clarity as I could study faces of unbridled rapture: holding a newborn baby, a pensive bride, a proud grandfather. The heart expressing the borderless, inclusive language of human emotion.

I am no stranger to photography. Dad had practically invented the camera, sending in his prototypes of various film apparatus to Kodak when he was just ten years old. In portraits of me as a toddler, my chubby hand was often clutching a light meter, the nearest toy to keep me busy. After my father died, it became clear that he was truly a photographer, trapped in the body of an insurance broker. The countless carousels of Kodachrome slides in perfectly orchestrated arrangements providing the evidence.

The gift of this book of photos opened me to something riveting: a woman praying, a man working a steel mill, a meaningful embrace. My eyes fixed on my species, I peered into the souls of which I longed to deeply understand.

Though it was not my planned vocation, I simply could not resist what I called a hobby. Workshops in Santa Fe and classes in a darkroom, while training my eye to notice what mattered deeply to me kept me intoxicated with direction. By the time I had babies, I was setting up a professional studio. Still studying documentary images and creating a love story under lights.

Not photographing hurt. When I was shooting, developing, printing, or framing, my soul found armistice. Watching children grow without capturing the changing spill of freckles was like losing a piece of Mom's china. Conversely, when I could push myself to look authentically, thwarting hesitation or chagrin, I felt a deep sense of artful purpose.

I listened now to mister craggy-no-teeth-man and snapped away, filling my thirsty cup.

Climbing back on the bus, I felt a familiar satisfaction like that of catching a fish or putting up preserves. I was reminded of Dorothea Lange, a photographer who'd documented Americans during the Depression. She'd sworn that she was not an artist but simply a documentarian, yet she'd trusted her heart to see people and did not put the lens cap back on until she'd captured her story.

I settled into my seat on our lorry, clutching my camera like a child would her Halloween candy, and opened my heart.

"You have purpose," soothed the voice. "There are stories in you that will bring you closer to your kin. Your job is to stay open. There is a divine plan for you."

As the bus ferried us back to Dublin, I felt a brief sabbatical from my bewilderment. My heart nudged me to explore, meditate, and, most importantly, eat something immediately. The best choice was, naturally, O'Donoghue's.

It was to be my last evening in Ireland, and I wanted to give her a fair goodbye. While devouring yet another delectable meat pie, I let the timeless Celtic musical stories make a home in my nerve center.

I was called "Noreen" in this gathering house by my new friends who swore it was no mistake that my father had named me such, as I was incontestably Irish at heart.

"My father swore he was Dutch," I told old Sean, who'd started the "shit the bed" chant evenings ago.

"He'd not been allowed music in his home growing up as a Protestant. Yet, he frequently snuck over to his friend's house to listen to the player piano that had but one roll, *Noreen, My Irish Queen.* Dad knew in his heart that music couldn't possibly be a sin."

"Your father was right, Noreen." Sean said with a wink, breathing a hot Guinnessy kiss on my forehead, "I think he led you here to the music. It's as close as he can be."

As if in a living cinema, the music was gentler that night. A new player was on the scene, a young, extraordinary beauty with brown curls down her back. She leaned between her legs an unwieldy harp so large that I wondered how she transported it with her delicate body. As her fingers danced across the strings, my heart swelled. Beside her was a man with a flute unlike any you'd see in the States, more like a recorder or fife. Many of the songs I didn't understand as she mostly sang in the Shelta dialect, but in some way, they spoke to me, like a mother's lullaby.

After several songs, I rose to leave and was caught by Sean.

"Wait, Noreen. One more for you."

I found the clairvoyance of these taproom tenders fascinating. Like a perfect shepherd dog in waiting, another glass of ale was set on the bar for me. It took very little prodding to keep me in comfort.

The young beauty rested her gaze on me as she theorized her last tune. She was reading me. We had not spoken but she'd sensed the power that her music was having on me and knew her duty well.

She started a slow, rippling *pling* that felt like the ocean tide, repeating the wash like a remedy. My mind drifted to the sensation of selchies and sirens in a dark ocean, down a deep cliff: unreachable but profoundly present. When she began to sing, I knew it immediately. I could hardly believe the magnitude of her gift.

I'd seen Sarah McLachlan some months back at a crowded venue with Mike in Berkeley. Yet the meaning of her song "Angel" at that time was simply lying in wait for this moment. I hadn't been ready then.

Now it was as if she was narrating my life. I had spent all my time waiting for another chance. I was still waiting for a break to make it okay. I didn't feel good at the end of the day and Ireland was supposed to provide some distraction. I longed to release the memories of Mike and float weightless in peace tonight.

There was a pause as I waited for the important chorus. The harpist's eyes met mine with the instructions to listen to her promise. My hands joined like a lifted cup, and breathed in her words with a deep inhale, taking each one inside me.

Listening to this woman sing about the arms of an angel pulling me from the wreckage, I did find some comfort. At least temporarily.

Women, I swear.

They're everywhere. I know, because I am one. I hope one day I can be such a soothsayer. Pitfalls are unavoidable, but we've got women. Rehearsing, enduring, sharing, and comforting. A taciturn colony of mermaids, quietly brushing one another's hair, reciprocating the timeless ritual of Mother Earth's magic sweetgrass.

I was thoroughly baptized when the time came to leave Ireland and face Mike in California, shabbily equipped with a heart full of fairy dust. Just one quick stopover in Reykjavik, Iceland, on my purple plane and I'd be home.

Finishing the Hat

It took a long time to get home.

The deal with WOW air was that one was able to fly to and from Europe for a ridiculously meager sum, but had to stop over in Iceland. This clever marketing was associated with the Icelandic tourism board. You could stay for an hour-and-a-half or a day-and-a-half. If you should choose to stay overnight, there were day trips available to the Blue Lagoon or a spectacular volcano. I'd opted for the hour-and-a-half layover both coming and going, as I'd no interest in leaving the airport. Yet, this layover was absorbed by some rumor of terrorist activity happening on my outbound flight. We were forced to disembark the grounded plane in Dublin and recheck our luggage. By the time we reached Reykjavik, the entire population of the plane had missed our connecting flights. It became apparent that I, along with all the other passengers, would be marooned for another day.

"Well, the good thing about Iceland is that there is a woman behind every tree," joked my seatmate, a retired Air Force man. "The bummer is there's not a tree to be found."

We waited in bewildering lines and were eventually bused to a deserted army bunkhouse with the promise of Domino's Pizza. Miles from anything, the storm we'd landed in was a whirling, freezing torrential rainstorm for which none of us was prepared.

Various hats, each portraying our previous expeditions—a French beret, a canvas Indiana Jones fedora, a wide-brimmed sun-shade, a wool beanie—all flew furiously from heads to puddles, then away from reach. Hair *tornado-ing* in confusion, strangers tried to stay calm as various soggy valises were manhandled from the bowels of the bus. As I noticed the passengers' collective resilience, I felt a sudden relief that Mike was not among us. I remembered his last scalding in public; he would no doubt have been a rageful embarrassment, and no help at all.

Exhausted, wet, and out of cigarettes, I surrendered to the bar to commiserate alongside my fellow refugees, half-heartedly awaiting our bunk assignments. Domino's never tasted so good, and as twenty-or-so-odd bunk fellows and I shared our stories and hilarious misadventures, our disorientation and discomfort graciously morphed into the reassuring comfort of human camaraderie.

Many of my contemporaries were going to miss work the next day, one, a wedding. I had less to lose than any of these folks, with nothing great to return home to. I relished the avoidance of the inevitable thud awaiting me back home, even if it meant I would have to endure the temporary dishevelment.

I opted to revel in the ridiculous. "Yes," I nodded to the bartender, "I'll have another."

My assigned lodging was a walnut-sized, solo room, the adjoining bath shared with four others. I washed my face, dried it with my soggy shirt, and soothed my skin with lavender oil. Cupping my hands over my face, I inhaled the comforting aroma of a perfect sticky flower bract as it drifted through my hypothalamus and landed gently in my memory center.

I'd purchased this oil in Lake Como as I awaited the arrival of Mike. Not having seen him in many weeks, I doused the sheets in anticipation. We'd had a lovely, romantic evening after his "welcome to our European journey dinner" in a town we now had in common with George Clooney. This was weeks before the unveiling of the Mortgage Broker.

In contrast to Lake Como, Iceland was austere. Warm, balmy, and inviting versus cold, foreboding, and terrifying. Holding the small vial with both hands up to my nose, as if it might hold a potion for curing confusion and tumult, I decided that lavender was not something I was ready to stop lov-ing. Living in it, though, was not possible for me at this time. The memories it evoked were too painful. Perhaps I could pay this sensation forward while I rode this imperative train of wisdom? I left the precious vial on the military base sink. Digging in my purple purse, I found a scrap of paper, a wadded receipt from some nefarious Italian purchase, and scrawled on it: *A gift for a fellow traveler. Please take it with you.*

I sunk into my skinny, stiff dorm bed. Pulling the starchy sheets and scratchy military blanket up to my chin, I opted to pray.

My belief in God is a strong net granted to me by my family. Fre-quently, the net feels too far from my gaze as I trapeze through changes, but it's there. Not a white-gowned man with tawny curls resting in puffy clouds, cradling a lamb, as superhero rays arch toward Earth. Rather, my God is a conclusive sensation of light and love and blackberries. As far back as the cambium of my reach is a solid assurance that should my world all fall apart, I will be taken care of.

If Grandpa were here, he might ask me about my walk with Jesus, which seemed to translate as: "Are you seeing the wonder?" Like Jesus, Grandpa Henry was a carpenter, a teacher, an artist, and a lover of all creatures, particularly children. A pioneer in Alaska with a team of dogs to get around, he and Grandma Pearl loved this life, never letting anything go unnoticed, or *un-thanked*.

Grandma made sure I knew the name of every botanical, to greet each flower blossom upon her arrival, as if I'd never before seen anything so remarkable. Likewise, Mother's devotion to flora was daffy.

"Pull over, Bud," she'd insist of my father, pointing out the window of the station wagon. "I have to get some of that *ceanothus*!" She'd then scale the side of the highway in her skirt and black leather dress boots, trowel in hand, and dig up a public plant.

It is this proclivity that has me always equipped with garden supplies in my car, eyes darting around at neighborhood lilacs and protea as I drive.

"It's good for the bush," I tell my friends when I show up with a bou-quet harvested from the neighborhood.

This awe of life and nature made the difficult feel surmountable, as if there were a larger plan for everything, and our most important job was to watch closely, trusting we had the best seat in the house.

"A problem? Bring it to prayer," Grandma often advised, as she'd stretch my tiny arms into my art smock. "Draw me the ocean."

This night I silently pondered, studied, and examined my predicament, then whispered to my God, "I'm lost. *God*, I'm really lost."

From the abyss came, "Yes. Are you seeing the wonder?"

I inhaled the lavender on my own face and fell into a dream. I was in a garden of zinnias and stargazer lilies. The ground was wet and warm. I dissolved into the center of a dinner-plate-sized dahlia and felt the comfort of my grandparents, my parents, and my own steady soul.

The following morning, the bus returned us to the empty, arctic airport where we waited for our connecting flights back to America. One of the previous night's compatriots broke the cold silence with a welcome folly, proudly donning a woman's sun hat he'd found in the parking lot. Another gal passed around the short movie she had made with her cell phone on Snapchat. It documented our ludicrous twenty-four hours of commotion, a terrorism threat that grounded our plane, and our mini, military-bunk friendships.

I felt ready to be home, set my bags down, and crawl into bed next to my Scoundrel. Or was he mine? I fantasized that my return would be greeted with an apology and a warm chest to rest my head on. There was so much to sort out and repair.

"I'm sorry," he would croon. "All I want to do is hold you."

This was not going to happen, and I knew it. This metaphorical lit candelabra that I'd been balancing on my forehead for so many years had fallen, leaving a glistening, waxy scar on my bare shoulders, matching the scars on my forearms from cliff-diving in Positano with Mike and the kids, just weeks earlier.

When at last I made it to San Francisco International Airport, I discovered the phone I'd purchased in Rome (as mine had been pick-pocketed in the crowded streets) didn't operate in the States. I borrowed a stranger's device on the BART train to let Mike know I was close. At 9:30 a.m., he'd be just getting his coffee and climbing back into bed with the paper, anxiously awaiting the mundane thrill of the garbageman. I could just climb in, poke my head under his arm, and listen to him narrate the newspaper.

"Listen to this," he'd speak softly as my head lay on his curly-haired chest. Donald Trump had recently announced that he was going to run for the presidency. Scoundrel and I had waxed on for months on the absurdity of the notion, and we agreed that the news had become a circus.

As the BART train rattled and swayed, emerging from the underwater tunnel separating San Francisco and Oakland, my ears popped. I watched the familiar West Oakland spin by. The Crucible, 12th Street, MacArthur, the California Hotel—all as familiar as the balmy and breezy hometown weather.

I'd spent many years studying Oakland and her history, and felt quite equipped to challenge just about anyone to a story duel. The old Victorian structures of downtown were my friends, and although many parts of the metropole had been riddled with crime and poverty, this was a place I understood. The Gold Rush, transcontinental railroad, Kaiser Shipbuilding, Pullman Cars, and the rich jazz scene make my multicultural home a place to feel deliciously proud of. I breathed in the renewed sensation of the homey calico palette unique to Oakland.

When the doors opened at my Rockridge Station, I was welcomed with the familiar, warm, and breezy October of my home. Everything felt friendly and yielding, with the exception of Mike, who was angry that I was a day late. Somehow, that had cramped his style.

His tone was startling. "Get in the car! Why doesn't your phone work? Are you an idiot?"

I'd almost forgotten Scoundrel's lack of grasp and filter on his temper. Yet, I stepped right into my bob-and-weave routine, the necessary tool to dodge his thrust.

"If my phone not working means I am an idiot, then I suppose I am," I murmured.

Had I forgotten that my lover entirely lacked emotional intelligence, or had his mounting disinterest happened over time? Like a slowly boiling frog not recognizing the increasing heat of fatality, maybe the time away from Mike starkly revealed how easy life could be when I wasn't navigating around his impatient rants. Or maybe he was a neat guy, but just for a while, and when his need to move on came, he had to make his signals clear.

How could anyone endure this? Why had I?

As we climbed up the hill to his house, I noticed a metallic department-store aroma in the cab of his Lexus, causing me to squirm. He explained that he and Kate Mortgage Broker had decided to make a go of things and that I needed to work on moving out. I worried about this girl/woman, as she seemed very demanding, but this choice was one made for me. My

Scoundrel wanted her, or felt some satisfaction in her needing him. I, at this point, needed to reconfigure my nest.

Settling back into stateside life took some time. My phone, set on a Roman plan, required the smartest person at the Apple Genius Bar several days to de- and re-code. I was booked to photograph a pregnancy session of another one of the players' wives of the Golden State Warriors, and I had work to do. Coming back to loading and lighting and learning new clients felt like holy ground, but I had accidentally left the second camera that I'd bought for the trip at the army base in Iceland. I didn't need it, but I wanted it back. Being separated from any gear was unsettling.

What I did need was space and time to regroup, to find my footing in this new scenario.

Now that Scoundrel's proverbial spilled beans were scattered for all to see, it was easy for him to spend most of his time with his new lover. I learned she had three children, not just one, in Orinda—a land through the "culture-shock" tunnel. A land I know well as my family moved me there after middle school to keep me safe, ostensibly to improve our demographic. Though only five miles west of Oakland, the nature of this valley embodies the sultry climate of pools, barbeques, several Visa cards in every wallet, and a sea of minivans. In short . . . bland white people.

When sudden wealth had moved my family to this valley in 1975, we went from buying bell-bottoms at Fowlers Western Wear to The Little Daisy and I. Runway models came to the house flaunting the latest fashion choices. My father had worked hard selling insurance and bringing stability to the dust-bowl, migrant population of Richmond, California. His goal to provide the best life he could for our family had moved my pubescent self to the East Bay enclave. Cars and houses were Daddy's way of expressing his love. Life was comfortable there; heck, we had a built-in swimming pool. I do remember, though, missing the multicultural melting pot of my childhood friends and the savory, down-to-earth comfort of a textured kind of people. Now Mike slotted right into his new family in this sunny life of luxury, thus graciously allowing me the time I needed to make the best decision for myself as to where to go.

Home seemed a suitable answer, but where was that now?

Domicile

"I have a house" would be an understatement. Like Isak Dinesen mused on having a song for Africa but questioned whether Africa had a song for her, I wondered whether I could ever get back home. My financial nest egg was the Oakland Hills house my first husband Stephan and I had feathered so lovingly and extravagantly in the fat years. At twenty-five, I received an inheritance that made me a catch for marriage and made the remodeling choices easy. Basically, "all the best, please."

Stephan had been my universe. Tall, elegant, and slender as the western depiction of Jesus, he fancied himself a musical celebrity in the New Wave scene of San Francisco. He wore his hair greased high like a rooster comb on stage, but down and long otherwise, giving him a boyish, hippy charm.

When our social diagrams *venned* at a weekend beach-house party, I was immediately taken by his ability to know and do just about anything. We sat in the too-large ceramic bathroom on the ledge of a gigantic bathtub, our legs dangling in the warm water and conversed for hours about music, family, fashion, history, and our dreams for the future. The people we had come to the party with—my current squeeze and his—were passed out on quaaludes in loungers on the beach. I drove him home in my Datsun B210 so we could talk further, leaving our partners at the beach house to fend for themselves.

I was twenty-three and just back from New York where I'd been modeling the summer swimwear line in the frigid Big Apple winter. I'd returned to California by request; my mother had complained that something wasn't right, and requested that I come home. I was doing some two-bit acting, working days as a filing clerk at an office, and evenings, I was serving up cocktails at a country and western dive bar. The bar was not far from the warehouse Stephan had transformed into a recording studio. He found it natural to frequently linger at my bar, seating himself by the drink-well and chatting with me. I could feel his eyes on my tight, white corduroys and denim blouse as I served up whiskey and Bud Light to the urban cowboys. It was exhilarating.

Steph came on very strongly. "Encore" was scrawled on a note I found on my pillow the first time he spent the night. Within the course of a few weeks, I had a musical promotional flyer photo of him with his rooster hairdo under my clear plastic blotter at the office. When questioned, I would tell people, "That is the man I will marry."

My return from New York still fresh, I'd rented myself a tiny apartment nearby and hovered closely to my empty-nesting folks. Mom was seeing a slew of medical specialists to discern her medical intuition, while Dad, after thirty years of marriage, was writing love letters extolling his rejuvenated crush on his wife. How-to books with titles like, *I'm OK—You're OK*, *What Color Is Your Parachute?*, and *Love Under Repair* littered the house. Fawning over her like a puppy, I would find a note from Dad in Mom's car. "I have washed and detailed your car as a token of my deep respect and enduring love for you."

I, though, was falling in love with a dynamic jack-of-all-trades who seemed to imbue me with every talent I needed. I followed his band in South of Market clubs like a groupie in my mini skirt and leg warmers, dancing late into the night, eating dinner at the famed Hamburger Mary's dive-diner at 3:00 a.m. I often called in sick to my office job.

"It's ovarian cancer." Mom sat me down at the antique table in her breakfast nook. "But I believe wholeheartedly that it is not part of God's plan that I die, so I don't want you to worry." Having been a voluptuous woman, Mom's diminishing weight was becoming increasingly alarming. She was barely forty-nine years old.

In complete denial, I continued my party of distraction, ignoring the blood-filled tissues I'd find in the bathroom trash cans. Within six months, my two older siblings were called in from other states and we gathered around her in a hospital bed that she'd been inhabiting for less than a week.

Mom had fallen into a coma and was no longer responding. When we all arrived, we gathered closely, all hands on her limp body. The hospital room was surreal. Mundane objects, like food trays of untouched fruit cups, cheery cards, and airborne dust particles seemed to swirl weightlessly around us.

"She knows we're all here," Dad sobbed.

Above her clear oxygen mask, a tool imploring her to breathe, her eyes opened. She rendered a long gaze with each of us for several lengthy moments. It was too late to ask her to stay.

Tears streamed down our mother's cheeks. So blue were her eyes. So well had I known them. How deeply I had relied on them. How fondly I had laughed with them. When she closed them at last, Dad, cradling her head with both hands, laid his forehead on hers, and let out a wail like I had never, and will never, hear again.

The Earth cracked open at that moment. I could feel the molten light erupt in a fiery comet. I closed my eyes, but the light remained visceral. It was profoundly blinding and strangely comforting.

Pay attention.

The following year was a blur. An ocean of people had to tell me how wonderful my mother had been and how enormous the loss was. I was acutely aware of these observations, and frequently felt that I needed to comfort others more than they did me, but my father's needs were far too great to afford time to dwell on the grief.

Mom's spirit lingered close by, depositing incandescent miracles. Without her cumbersome body, she could move swiftly, dolloping pearls of epiphany-like seagull poop. Signs of her were unavoidable and all-consuming. The face of a flower, a cluster of ladybugs, relentless owls, and my dreams. The constant dreams of a warm hand pushing on my forehead, swelling my palate with the weightless feeling of suspension, like floating in amniotic fluid. This meditative state of mind was one I could, over time, conjure. I had salvaged her silky blue nightgown and kept it in a large

Tupperware container under my bed. I could pull it out anytime to revisit her offering of comfort, wrapping the gown around my pillow and burying my head in her imaginary bosom.

Dad was an inconsolable cataclysm. He couldn't work or eat, pacing from room to room as if he might turn the corner and find her standing at the sink, pulling leaves off tulip stems in careful design of her weekly floral arrangement. I was the closest to home, so I took on the role of Mother, accompanying him to award ceremonies honoring his years of success.

"It's all a charade," he moaned as we got into the car for one such affair. He lay his forehead on the steering wheel, rocking it side to side.

"Dad, we're going to get through this." I felt ridiculous in my conservatively cut, navy-sequined dress, my hair curled to look like a twenty-year-ago rendition of his dead bride.

Turning to me, he looked small, like a young boy dressed up for a party he did not wish to attend. His imploring eyes were as blue as a robin's eggs. These eyes, too, had been a place of solid guidance, yet behind them I saw, not my hero, top sales member of the company round table. Behind them I couldn't find the spirit of the man that played melodica, dancing around the living room, stereo blasting. Behind them I saw terror. He'd lost his grip, dropped his basket.

"You don't understand!" he wailed, gasping for breath, now. "I didn't pay attention for all of these years. I neglected her. I was a selfish, cruel, and horrible husband. I can't live with myself. This is all my fault."

Looking back at photos of that event, and pretty much all images from that tenuous year, my father was clearly slipping away. Friends advised him to get through one year of birthdays and holiday traditions and he'd be fine. Psychologists gave him drugs. That, I recall, was a mistake. It was the mid-eighties, and since then we have come a long way with antidepressants. The combination he was on seemed to intensify his grief, making his company increasingly onerous.

A year and a week after we lost Mom, I came over to a house emitting a blaring security alarm and containing a dead father. To this day, I cannot hear so much as a car alarm without viscerally recalling that day.

After he'd craftily rigged a flexible hose from tailpipe to fuselage, Dad—what was left of my father—slumped defeatedly in the front seat of his car. Beside his prone body sat a tray with a silver water pitcher—the one we used for Thanksgiving—and a writing pad.

Yes, he'd left a note, a lengthy one, explaining why he had made this choice and directives on the choices we were now left to make. It was obvious he had worked for months formulating this plan. The trust, the cash, the stocks, the property, who was to get what, and navigational instructions for Ron, my eldest sibling, were carefully spelled out. If he had the ability to validate his own death certificate, he would have done so. Within six months, I had enough money to buy a house, maybe two. Naturally, Stephan proposed that we marry, which we did, sparing no expense.

Our wedding was elaborate, with 1920s Rolls-Royces shuttling our guests to a turn-of-the-century mansion. It was Steph's idea that we learn to scuba dive for our honeymoon so we could dive the Mariana Trench to mingle with monster clams large enough to climb in, like a mermaid and merman, and tempt out pearls the size of bocci balls.

In overalls and dusty ponytails, we immersed ourselves in doubling the size of a 1940 Craftsman gem. For three years, we jackhammered, paved, dug, sawed, chopped, sanded, painted, and planted. Balancing on joists, we pooed in the honeypot outhouse and survived on peanut butter and celery. Each night we made love on a mattress in the living room adjacent to the magic fireplace while sketching ideas . . . *what if this doorway were rounded?*

There, we conceived and raised Henry and Alice. I pause to sigh on the dreamy anamnesis of those thirteen years. As a stay-at-home hippy with the most important life goals in place—play, learn, love, teach, repeat—I flourished. We spent all of our days making and growing things, learning, and exploring every corner of our partial acre.

Song, story, poetry, and craft, dancing around and around the living room baby grand while Steph *staccatoed* ditties on the piano or blasted CDs of *The Sound of Music*, Peter, Paul and Mary, and Louis Armstrong. I felt completely in my element. The work was physical, purposeful, and full of animals.

Steph always had enormous ideas. After our castle was built, he would build a large company, acting as both CEO and CFO. The funding would be from my inheritance, of which he had full control. I had complete confidence in him and busied myself with the important work of home and children. I spent countless hours on hand-stamped wrapping paper, first-class Easter egg hunts, quilting, and holiday parties. I taught the children to cook, to sing, to make animals from tinfoil and papier-mâché. Stephan traveled, became dressier, and gradually came home with gigantic chrome watches and strange short haircuts.

When things fell apart, much to my overwhelming sorrow, our split turned into a dispute that somehow required us never to look into each other's eyes again. His two Hershey-brown targets that had guided me through the spiraling abyss and shattering loss of both parents, and ushered me into the joy of family, changed, and turned away from me. The smartest and funniest man in the room moved into another big house higher on the hill with an indoor play structure.

I was devastated. We were in court for an eternity, squandering time and money on our disappointment. *Raschke vs. Raschke* plied through four family court judges and several attorneys. We were on a first-name basis with the bailiff. I was eventually able to retain the home, the flimsy confidence of the kids, and a new tattered reality. When terrorists then obliterated the twin towers, I felt somehow understood, as if I were not the only person in the universe being blindsided.

A few years later, after the wounds of divorce had turned to scar, I met Paul on Match.com. He *tarzaned-in* from the Silicon Valley in the South Bay with his solid jaw and easy demeanor. When we first made love, I heard my heart crack. It was an actual sound that caused me to reach up and touch my chest to be sure my heart was still there. He had two great boys older by a few years than my children. Could we make this work?

Paul proposed to me with a big ring that felt unnatural on my rough, gardener's hands. It kept snagging on sweaters and loosening in dishwater. After a long day of weeding the garden, I checked the ring's status with my thumb and it was gone. I felt ashamed and irresponsible, but Paul was still there. When the day came to take our vows, we made do with a pawnshop diamond pavé that I wear to this day to remember what a good man he was. We married on a farm by the Eel River, and he bought me a banjo. Merging our families together in my house, we were the veritable Brady Bunch, complete with an Alice, but she didn't do windows or make six sandwiches every morning.

Together we wrangled four teenagers, two dogs, three cats, six chickens, and the economic downturn of 2008. Paul commuted hours to and from work to keep us afloat, massaged me physically and emotionally for ten years, then lost his job and his confidence. By the time all of the kids had grown and flown, there was little left but drunken arguments and depression. We tried to resuscitate the early years, yet the stress of his un-employment ate at us like a pack of hungry wolves.

It was unbearable to watch him fritter away his retirement money on my big house. Day after day, I watched his spiraling detachment from his corporate connections. There was no work to be had. Music, though, which he had previously studied, brought him solace. I gave him my banjo and hitched my wagon to the shiny object that promised me an easier ride—the Scoundrel.

Pushing the guilt aside was problematic. With helmets strapped on tight, my Scoundrel and I were touring the city in tiny yellow go-cars, laughing all the way, while Paul was in a dark corner dive on his fourth Sazerac. I met Paul occasionally at these bars where we would catch up on the happenings of the kids, tiptoeing around the truth—that I was an ass-hole. That I had literally walked off our sinking ship, rather than going down with him.

His kindness only made it worse.

When I moved in with said shiny object, Scoundrel, I had rented my home to young and successful filmmakers. Now, it would seem that the obvious thing after this European discovery of Ms. Mortgage Broker would be to evict them and move back to my large home.

Yet, the voice within me didn't line up with that plan. Rather, a sensa-tion came over me, telling me that I needed to lighten my load and explore. I let the "Snake Boyz," as I called my tenants (the house was situated on Snake Road), know about my breakup with Mike and that reclaiming my home was my end goal, yet it would probably be another year before I did.

I could find a room to rent in the meantime. Mike, at this point, was never home, and let me know I had two months to move out. Alice and Tinashe could stay six months. This felt more than fair to me.

I didn't know where I was to live, I needed to restore my work con-nections, and I was in the throes of confusion. This seemed like the worst time, thus, why not . . . a good time to start dating.

"I can't move back into my house," I thought, "until I can find a man to support me."

The Men Out There

Start with . . . *If you could have anything in the whole world* . . .

I often begin with this question when advising friends and family on life choices. This method seems to be effective in choosing a restaurant, an educational direction, shoes, or cheeses. You can't always get what you want, but knowing what you'd have if you aimed for it seems to make the journey more purposeful. In choosing my next man, I gave it a lot of thought. Opening the application on the dating site, OkCupid, I created my profile.

Me: mid-fifties, creative, single, photographer, and local historian in the Oakland Hills seeks a partner to adventure with and for a possible long-term relationship.

You: kind, tall, trustworthy, funny, and secure.

What I wanted, but didn't write, was a sex-starved fireman or guy with a PhD, half my age, that could build things, was on the verge of early retirement, and dying to take care of me. I rustled up some photos of myself that were fairly accurate and hit publish.

Then began my stint on OkCupid, where I was to date no less than seventy-five men, while living in a changing domicile and under the direction of a deteriorating government. I promised my heart would stay open to all lessons of light.

Still living at Scoundrel's, my first date's online handle was "Robertasaurus." A super creative appraiser who built much of his lower Oakland House with his bare hands, he had a five-year-old child with Down syndrome and was an art scene maven.

Rob really enjoyed me, and I, him. A not-very-tall-yet-solid-bodied man, he cruised through his life pretty comfortably, inviting me to classic rhythm-and-blues shows at Yoshi's and unusual parties at the Ghost Ship—an artist's commune that would later burn to the ground, killing many. I let him know that I was just beginning this journey and needed to stay open to seeing several people at once and leave intimacy to a minimum.

Rob was into astrology and felt that my Gemini qualities were wildly interesting, making doing my chart essential. No longer intimate with Mike, I leaned on Rob as a friend with benefits. Over time, we drifted. Like many of these men, he would surface occasionally to check in.

"Big Generator" lived in the Towers Emeryville and made deals. Tall and well-built, he worked out a lot and made a pretty mean fish sandwich. He drove a Corvette convertible, which I adored, yet he was often outspoken, and I wondered about his political leanings.

On our second date, I was able to assess this language as "humor," and upon further conversation, found him to be politically astute and operating on my side of the political and social spectrum. In a short while, he moved to Sonoma County, twenty miles north, to stay in a townhome he owned up there.

Gene called frequently, and treated me like a princess. Even while dating other women, he assured me I had the prize-winning *tuchus*.

"Tuchus?" I asked. "That sounds like a Hebrew word."

"Indeed." He grinned. "It means bottom." His bushy gray eyebrows lifted like a nimbus cloud, exposing a broad and jagged smile, as if he'd just coined a forbidden word, like fart.

Something felt oddly comfortable about my Gene.

Here was a man complimenting my ass, which, *feministly speaking*, should have caused some chafe. Gene was a friend. If I didn't feel comfortable, or perceived his language as inappropriate, I probably wouldn't be sitting at his kitchen nook. His extraordinarily loud musical forays made me laugh. Who doesn't love a man with a huge library of Broadway tunes?

Gene, though, never asked me to stay, nor would I have known what to do if he had. I enjoyed that he found me attractive, and that he fancied festive afternoon outings. Therefore, I continued answering his texts and lingered on his advancements, saying *yes* to adventures, knowing full well, as did he, that we weren't soul mates.

Keith, or "God's gift to women," and I met in a bar. He had a soft whistle in his voice and looked at my face the way Robert Redford cinematically looks at his love interests in film, scanning from top to bottom. He took me in like a dog eyeing beef jerky. If I could give any man advice on how to lure in a lady, that would definitely be one easy skill to adopt.

Keith had eyes like my grandfather, soft, yet solid, and when he so effectively stabbed me with them, and said, "I want to see you naked," my knees buckled. He lived in a condo in our village where we stole away.

It was epic. He ushered in lovemaking like a dancer, his eyes glued to mine.

We talked about the usual things: what happened to the marriage, tell me about the kids. He seemed caring, yet in the weeks following, his calls were generally about a *rendezvous sans* dinner—not much more than a booty call. I let him know that I would like to actually get to know him. But this was a classic case of getting the milk without buying the cow. It was clear that, out of lust, I'd made a mistake.

I saw him in the village here and there, and I often wondered how things would have gone had I been more elusive. A lesson learned, or rather, a lesson in the making.

Several dates with other OkCupid guys were one-time meetings—coffee, walks, or one glass of wine. I kind of fancied the retired sheep farmer that met me at the little farm to walk Jewel Lake. He disappeared, as did so many.

I drove way too far to the Delta to go on a thrilling speedboat ride with James who took off his sweatshirt to reveal a Trump T-shirt. *Done.*

Another Rob met me and a girlfriend at a pub and I literally nodded off while he went on and on about how his wife had let him down.

One guy who owned and operated a pizza place in downtown San Francisco shared a late-night slice with me.

Beautiful Othello owned a 1905 Victorian in the city which I longed to see, but he just kept falling off the radar, saying, "Oh yeah, you . . . we should get together." I mean, honestly, why even be on a dating site if you can't give it some energy?

In the elegant dark bar on College Avenue, one guy, Bill, revealed that he was bisexual and trying to stick with women for a while. Although I found him as handsome as Superman, we didn't really feel an attraction to each other and were frank about it. A week later, another bi man reached out and I gave him Bill's contact info. They hit it off and both thanked me.

My dear girlfriend, Dani, so-named as her father had hoped for a boy, was also single in her fifties, and we had, in our time, considered some kind of tandem life. Perhaps a spread somewhere entitled "The Golden Girl Ranch" with just one cowboy to service our needs and clean out the stalls. A bombshell blonde from my high school days, Dani and I reconnected at the funeral of a guy who'd been a lover to both of us at different times. He was the star quarterback. "I forgot how much I like you," Dani and I said to each other, and started walking together on crisp autumn mornings to share our goals and foibles.

"Men are odd," she often assured me.

A volunteer at the local animal shelter, Dani shared with me her training on understanding dogs via a color-coded collar system. It's quite elementary, and in my dating experience, I've found the categories work quite well for cataloging men.

A blue collar symbolizes timid. Many things can happen with a worried man, but generally, they disappear, even after a perfectly lovely first date. Perhaps these men are not really looking for a relationship, afraid of their own shadow, sadly damaged, or unable to recognize a plausible partner when it sits before them.

Green signifies friendly, gregarious, and fawny, following you from room to room. These men often feel certain right away that you are their master and whatever you want you may have. It is these men that for some reason are just not the sweet spot for me, and frequently become hurt and whimper on your welcome mat. Green collars can remain a friend for life, yet there is no fire.

Those donning orange collars jump up on you, guard their resources, and have difficulties with transitioning. Getting them out of their pen is an ordeal and they tend to go apeshit when another dog comes by. A dog with an orange collar (and sometimes a man with a similar designation) is aggressive and uses bullying as a relationship tactic. Arrogant and self-serving, these dogs are most apt to bite. These men are to be avoided at all costs.

Then, there is the purple collar, and this one is my imagination's figment, because only unicorns have purple collars. The perfect animal. Stunningly beautiful inside and out. Heart of gold and steady-tempered. Creative, a joy to be with, and can walk for miles just to be near you. I had a purple collar but once—his name was Rick, and he was a dog, not a man.

It was clear that the perfect guy had yet to come along. However, I was learning about the men out there and making new acquaintances. None had caused a butterfly feeling, but I knew, if patient, I would find him. I convinced myself that I was experiencing a stage of my foray that allowed me to experiment with my own reactions and sensations. I'd learned with Scoundrel how to tolerate a toxic environment, as playful as it was. "How did I feel about that? What is it you are looking for?" I asked myself. "Do you even know?"

The Great Kachink

On November 8, 2016, I asked Scoundrel if he wouldn't mind staying home with Alice and me for dinner so we could watch Hillary win the presidential election. Mike and I were aligned politically, working together on local affairs. Obama had been so good for us and we'd worried about the possibility of a shake-up. Hillary was not our first choice, but with Sanders out of the race, we knew she represented our democracy significantly better than the terrifying alternative.

We stuffed ourselves with Mike's delicious chicken enchiladas and settled in to watch the paint-by-number set fill in the landscape of our country. Blue, blue, blue, red, red, red, red. Red. RED!

Could this be happening? No, impossible! Donald Trump, a simple-minded land baron, could not be winning a presidential campaign. Mike glanced down at his phone and lifted his head in amazement. "Wow," he reported, "Mortgage Broker voted for Trump."

KACHINK!

Kachink is one of my made-up words; I have a few. I started making up words as a child. *Qumer* (pronounced cue-mer) defines those things that are adorable, particularly pertaining to an endearing elderly person or couple, or small, delectable things, such as tiny carrots or baby toes. Mister craggy-teeth man in Ireland was most certainly *qumer*, as are kittens. *Zom* is a simply perfect thing, like a lemon cake, an old car, or a perfectly orchestrated event. *Zom-Bom* is an accentuated *zom*. A *kachink*, now, is an emotionally audible epiphany, a sudden realization. Like one of those "wait, what was I thinking? *Oh*, now I get it" moments.

My head spinning, I dropped my fork on my plate as Alice gave me her "don't say anything" eyes.

"What on earth?!" I detonated. "You mean that was something you hadn't asked her?"

I stormed out of the room and into the bathroom, slamming the door behind me. Sitting on the closed toilet seat, I rested my head in my hands. Tears burned my eyes as I instinctively waited for Mike to come to the door and implore me to come out. This, I knew, would not happen. His desire for this woman was greater than his values.

Kachink went my heart. It was suddenly clear that a whole lot of people were going to need to do a whole lot of things to safeguard our people, our nation, and our planet, and my sweet Scoundrel was on a different side. This couldn't be true. Mike was a lot of things, but uninformed was not one of them. He read the paper. He watched the news. He formed educated opinions. He was a smart guy.

I had no choice but to come out of the bathroom. Feeling like a defeated child after a tantrum, I returned to the sofa, and opted for a different, more empathetic tactic.

"Mike," I said, searching his eyes, "this man is talking about building a wall between the US and Mexico."

"I think she just didn't know who to vote for," he said in her defence.

"Why would you go out with someone who doesn't know who to vote for?" I scolded him.

Mike averted his eyes with his now commonly used "it doesn't really matter" expression.

Mike's eyes were dark and tender. He'd once told me that after betraying his last girlfriend, she had described them as "lying and beady eyes."

I will not do that, I resolved. He is my Scoundrel. I will always love his dark and tender eyes.

The revelation that his relationship with Mortgage Broker was more important to him than his political compass was evident now. Understanding this would be helpful in further moving me through this confusing separation.

So many of life's tectonic shifts are instrumental for growth. The key is to keep dancing on this Earth, straddling the chasm, debasing as much personal catastrophe as possible.

Alice set her hand on mine. With her touch, I knew what she was gently transmitting: "He's not worth it."

Stretching my head backward, it was welcomed by the headrest behind me. An instinctive, deep breath filled me with oxygen, replacing the pain of tension that I hadn't even known was there. The antique crisscrossed skis mounted high above me on the terra-cotta wall astride the river rock fireplace brought me a respite of pleasure. Color and form has always had that effect on me.

When I first moved in with Mike, his house was an artless eyesore. His wife had left him twenty years prior, grinding all home care and creative nesting activity to a halt. I recalled finding a single Mexican blanket with a splash of soothing color, and while draping it over our bed, I'd thought, "Yes, I can do this. I can make this place fabulous."

"You go, girl," he'd said at the time, "this is our house."

I had painted all the walls beautiful earth tones and threw out the eighties window valances, moldy shower curtains, and old boxes of unused Pampers. I repaired the dryer and sliding glass door that had been broken for decades. Mike's underwear was carefully folded in a Duncan Phyfe dresser below an adorned wall with three antique mirrors, watch fobs, and his baby picture. I was the instigator of tearing out three walls to transform this poorly designed house into a palace with this great room and a new deck extending off the kitchen. Mounting those skis ten feet up was no bunny trail, but it was just the right item to finish the room, and we loved them.

"My work here," I resolved, "is done." My benevolence had been squandered.

I'd believed, somewhere in my heart, that Mike would note these decorating merits and find me a perfect partner to grow alongside. I was developing us, which would keep me safe from falling into poverty and loneliness. There was no way for me to take care of myself and I'd blindly and deftly pretended that things were running smoothly. Would Mortgage Broker move in here and make love to Mike in the outdoor shower I'd designed? Had she already?

I had invested value in this relationship that had always been destined to sink. Now it was upon me to elegantly curtsy out in the most efficient way so as not to cause any further losses: the club membership, the leased car, our adjoining workplace, not to mention our tattered-yet-long-built friendship. For Christ's sake, I was still living there.

I'd wrapped up relationships before and had some experience. It could be done right; it could be done wrong. One could kick a dead rapport and throw plates or one could calmly know one's own name and maneuver on with dignity and gratitude. Here I was, determined to experiment with supreme kindness, empathy, and support, and watch the results.

I crouched on the floor in front of Mike and laid one hand on each of his hairy knees. Looking up into his eyes, he was forced to look at me.

"You can teach her."

Alice rubbed the back of her ear and twisted her mouth with a "yeah, right" expression, then stood to clear our plates. She knew I was doing this to buy more time. When I joined her in the kitchen, she set the plates down and gave me a hug. The two of us still enfolded, she whispered in my ear: "This is ridiculous. You gotta get out of here. You don't need to bow to that child. He fucked you over, Mom."

"I know." I rocked our hug.

It seemed like twenty minutes ago that I'd rocked this little girl to sleep, singing Nordic lullabies to send her off. Her head of golden curls, her upturned nose like Dr. Seuss' Cindy-Lou Who were unbearably dear. How could I have known twenty-five years would pass and she would be so brilliantly supportive of me so late in life?

"Thank you, Alice." I sighed.

What Were You Thinking?

Around Christmastime, Tess, my friend in high school and roomie in college, lost her father, Bill. Bill and Marty Forrester were deeply a part of my high school and college timeline, so attending the memorial was essential.

There I stood, in the glorious Forrester house in bucolic Orinda, surrounded by Marty's amazing flower arrangements. I'd taken the opportunity to eulogize Bill for the friends, family, and grandchildren, talking about life at the Forrester's in the late seventies.

Swimming in pools without sunscreen, while listening to Jackson Browne and Rolling Stones records, tony advertising executives sprawled about, doling out wit and wonder. The house was always unlocked. Unembarrassed ashtrays brimmed with half-smoked Dunhills, while several convertibles relaxed in the driveway, keys dangling from the steering columns.

Bill Forrester was a marketing genius, and to his credit, the nicest person in any room. I recalled watching Johnny Carson on TV while Bill sat with Tess, soothing her gently, while she comfortably snuggled with him in an affectionate, casual, father-daughter way. When I was sixteen, Marty taught me her famous rice dish, with broth, onions, and lots of butter, which I use today to the delight of dinner guests.

It was at this lovely memorial gathering where I met Betsy. A friend of Marty's and in her seventies, Betsy listened in at the girls' table to my story of Europe, where I'd lost Scoundrel. She loved my storytelling and I was fascinated watching her hands as she spoke, because she was missing the two central digits of her left hand. When she asked if I'd like to walk around the reservoir with her on Sunday, I naturally said yes. "I'll meet you under the flag."

When I arrived the Sunday following the memorial, I was dressed for a walk: no makeup, a baseball cap, and yoga pants. I was surprised to discover she had brought a colleague, well, actually her son—John. We walked about a hundred yards, three miles short of the full hike, when she said, "Okay, then, these knees are done. I'm going to go home."

John was cute, and most notably, tall, and we both laughed about the obvious setup. Approximately my age, he lived in Hawaii, where he managed property, or money, or something. An hour walk around a reservoir was a nice way to get acquainted. He had four grown daughters strewn from here to there and was home for the holidays to celebrate with them and his parents in Lafayette. He shared stories of his childhood in this oaky valley, and I told him of mine. He confided that his wife had left him for a woman, had torn the whole castle down, sold the property, then changed her mind and asked if she could be with him again. Nordic, like I was, John exuded a softness that I wanted to fold myself into, or at the very least, touch.

We did not touch, but I felt a spark that couldn't contain the "if you have any time free while here" outreach.

Two days later, I found a phone message from a strange number announcing that John had lost his phone, yet he'd like to meet me for a drink at the Claremont, in Berkeley, on Tuesday.

Nobody says no to a drink at the Claremont Hotel. When I called the number back, it belonged to a golfing buddy who was no longer golfing with John, so I texted Betsy.

> Tell John yes to Tuesday and if he needs to borrow a stranger's phone, give him my number.

He can borrow my phone

Great. Now we were communicating through Mom.

The towering Claremont Hotel was built in 1915, and it encapsulates everything I care about as an historian in these parts. When I arrived, I immediately gravitated to the Hillary Tenzing Room, an homage to Edmund Hillary, the first person to climb Mount Everest, and his sherpa, Tenzing Norgay. In this room, with its dark mahogany wainscoting, I viscerally feasted with relish on tables piled high with fragrant old books and archaic climbing equipment. Inhaling the wonderful musk of *yesterland*, I ordered a scotch and dove in. John found me and ordered a matching malt.

The conversation flowed easily as I told him the things I knew about history, this place and that, painting words and stories of the Victorian era when women wore corsets and long skirts while they scaled mountains. It warmed me that, though he lived in Honolulu, this was home to him, and that his parents had an old ranch in a place I found familiar.

Yes! Here is what I was looking for: to be back in my home with a strong man that embraced the real me. This lovely man was intelligent and genuinely interested in what I had to share. I entertained the thought that perhaps I had found a solid replacement for my heart with ease and without a long waiting period. A smooth transition from a prankster to a broad-shouldered man in a button-up. I liked the idea of it. Naturally, it would be someone from my second hometown in the valley, as we would have so much in common. Though many of the people I'd left back home were complacent and flat, lazy from easy security, perhaps it was the island life that gave John more dimension.

After some appetizers and a few remember-me deep kisses, I asked him if he might like to come over to my place to continue our conversation. His "yes" reminded me, with a hot fiery pang, that I had no home.

"Perhaps you'd like to see my photo studio?" I backpedaled.

My studio is, in truth, an office with a kitchen and a ceiling high enough to hold three studio lights. It wasn't my space alone, but shared part-time with a guitar instructor and my Scoundrel—another thing we'd need to un-tease. Mike had a license to appraise property, though he didn't work very frequently. He had found the space particularly for me when he'd been in love with me. I felt sure no one would be there at this late hour, so we stole away among the lighting stands and cables.

Within moments of unlocking the door, we were on the floor, swimming in a gray mottled backdrop, panties flying everywhere. I surrendered into what I knew to do with someone unfamiliar. These hands were larger, shoulders, broader. I generally find solace in a familiar soul mate, but my hunger was clear, and the strangeness of the circumstance was provocative. I was ravenous to feel attractive to a real man, and here, I had one. I sensed in John a similar urgency, and after borderline violent intercourse, I cradled his head on my breast and quietly wept relief.

A connection to another spirit, my heart near another's. The vulnerability cracked me wide open. Engulfing myself in the moment, I begged the sensation to stay.

John left early and I awoke with that feeling.

Now remember, to say I'd been dating would be an understatement. For several months, I'd been meeting an average of three men a week, and on occasion, three in a day—coffee with one gent, a walk with another, and dinner with yet a third. It's a shame I wasn't running for office with the campaign trail I was crusading. Actively seeking a partner, I was crafting a bouquet garni of friends. But this was different.

A crush. The dizzy-dancing, painful pull of yearning. "Call Me," I urged through the universe. "I will put a spell on you to make you want me." The chemical dance, pulsing deep in the DNA, imploring another's heart to feel like mine. I breathed slowly into my hope of true intimacy. This man could be the answer to my dilemma.

When I was a girl awakening to her interest in boys, I wasn't quite sure why I wanted them to notice me. As if on cue, we were chasing boys around the playground for absolutely no reason other than we were children needing to run. What would we do if we caught a boy? Tie him up, tickle him, punch him? Maybe say something forever harmful. I don't think we thought that far. We were eight years old, still bringing blankies and transitional bears to slumber parties where we would splurge on Nestle's Quik.

By age ten, I fantasized that a boy in my school, Dino Granzelo, with his classic Sicilian mop of silky black curls over brilliant blue eyes, would ask to walk me home. His family started the garbage collection company in our borough, another immigrant dust-bowl family forming our town of Richmond. There, in front of our postwar suburban bungalow, he would pay attention to me, I mused. Why did I want this?

I just did.

By sixteen, the heat was on. Like an animal reaching juvenile status, my unquenchable desire was to get outside at night. Sixteen meant we could drive. It meant eight-track players in our new private apartment on wheels. Boys were an inevitable part of this new freedom. We liked spending hours grooming and posing for boys. They, in return, were walking boners. Needless to say, they figured it out before we did. I was an emotional ship at sea searching for a harbor.

This crush on John recalled these feelings. There really was no way to contact him, to let him know how strongly I was feeling without reaching out to his mother, who mustn't know how forward my behavior had been.

> Hi Betsy, would you tell John thank you for the wonderful evening. Should some more time free up for him, please let me know.

Later that afternoon, he phoned me to let me know that *yes*, we had a lovely experience and *no*, he couldn't see me because he was booked solid for the remaining week in California. "I'll call you when I visit again."

Sigh. "Why am I doing this?" I questioned myself. Men are simply different creatures than I am. I felt as if I would give up a tooth to talk to this man who was tugging at my heart, and he somehow brushed the experience off like a soggy raincoat.

Weeks later, I was standing over the sink in Scoundrel's kitchen, eating cottage cheese out of the tub, feeling sorry for myself. Cottage cheese was the only thing I could eat—that, and pears. Everything else was too much work for the funk I was in.

Mike was attending a Bruno Mars concert with Mortgage Broker. "What fifty-seven-year-old man follows Bruno Mars, a teeny-bopper pop star?" I chastised myself. "I suppose one who is dating a significantly younger woman." I pictured him purchasing gaudy gold chains and sunglasses to wear to the event, and somehow knowing all of the words to his songs. The sun was beginning to set, and although it had been raining for weeks, there was a break in the action, so I opted to walk out on the new deck to watch the spectacular show of orange and pink. I can always find a profound comfort in nature's beauty, eclipsing even the largest doubts.

"I'll take it!" I thought, breathing in the clean, damp air. I was so happy not to be in a crowded mosh pit of a concert hall, awaiting a barely-five-foot pop star to gyrate to some hit I didn't understand or care to hear. And, look, I could smoke a cigarette with nary a put-down. I reached for a cigarette, knowing Mike detested the habit, and inhaled it along with the evening. Perhaps I'll entertain myself with the dating site.

When I returned indoors, my cell phone, waiting for me by the sink, was illuminated with a message from John.

> I've got a new phone.
> Come to Honolulu. You
> don't have any reason to
> stay at your old
> boyfriend's house in the
> rain.

I thought about it for about forty seconds. I'm a Gemini and an impulsive one. I don't always make the wisest financial decisions, but tend to pursue what feels right at the moment. This trip would set me back close to a thousand dollars, and considering the needs at hand, this was a mistake. I walked out on the deck for another smoke. The air was wintery and waterlogged, my feet and mood were cold, and had been for weeks.

"You feel a crush and you need to explore it," my heart said. "You can do post-production work anywhere on a laptop. Your goal is to explore. Say yes."

Extinguishing my butt in the abalone shell teetering on the edge of the railing, I assured myself that the mother-of-pearl finish in my ashtray, echoing scenes of tropical breezes, was my go-light. I booked my flight and a room at the Aston Waikiki, six floors up, with a view of the ocean.

Three days later, the plane deboarded outside on the tarmac in Honolulu, and the balmy, *plumerian* seventy-six degrees felt floral and sweet on my battered heart. As I trotted down the air-stairs to the ground, I wanted to wave at imaginary cameras flashing in my face, welcoming me to my new life of sandals and outdoor lunches.

The hotel was perfect, and after dropping my tiny day bag in my room, the primary objective was to lose my socks and race, slow-motion, into the ocean.

"Do you need anything else?" the tawny man at the front desk asked.

"What kind of a question is that?" I beamed, grabbing not one but two hotel towels.

The sand was warm and inviting. My toes had atrophied from weeks in rain boots and I crashed full-force into the ocean, allowing her to tumble me silly.

Oceans.

Warm and turquoise ones, icy gray and rough ones, dangerously ominous ones, night oceans teeming with the threat of sharks. Cool rewarding ebb and flow on sunburned toes on a hot, sandy shore. I've never met a beach that hasn't completely enveloped me. The waves whisper and crash over and over as beautiful and unpredictable as a stage act, the admission always free. All I needed to do was show up.

A visit to any shore always requires a full day afterward to comb through my hair after either tossing in curls of tropical waves or enduring violent northern winds in a parka and hiking boots. The sound and sensation of the ocean, wherever I find myself, is just that: sensational.

"Bring your problems here," she says. Regardless of the other plans I may have made, she always calls me back to her side to share some mysterious secret and fill me with an awe bigger than anything one could ever buy.

The one given to me this late morning was the warm and blue kind, with floral undertones—a real favorite. The smell of sunscreen wafted from nearby laughing children, assuring me that I'd made a good choice.

Uncovering my phone from my towel, I lay in the hot sun and reached out via text to John.

> I'm here.

I was surprised by how quickly he responded, as if he gave a damn.

> Oh great. I've booked us
> dinner at the Duke and a
> sunset cruise for
> tomorrow, but your hotel
> has the best tiki bar so I'll
> meet you there for the
> sunset. How is 6:00?

That evening, I blissfully shimmied into a skirt, low-cut blouse, and, for the first time in years, heels. Heels are scarce in my closet, as I stand 5'9" without them, and with them, strangers regard me with sympathy and concern for the pain on my face. I don't understand them, but I'd packed these as I was anticipating a tall man (at last) and uncomfortable shoes seem to turn some men on. Thus, I'd give them a go.

When John met me in the bar, my heart soared. He was more handsome than I'd remembered, and as I stood and seesawed on my pedestals, he greeted me with a long and wonderful kiss. We measured up just fine. We sat and conversed about his job, my work, our families, and mutual friends back home over sticky mai tais.

"This is going to be a perfect long weekend away," I thought. "Nobody knows where I am or what I am doing. I can work virtually if need be. I can lay in my crisp hotel sheets all morning long if I want. If I have a friend to revel in a plate of pineapple there, well, so be it."

Folding my legs over his to expose my painfully high leather sandals, I whispered, "The view is better upstairs."

Indeed, it was, and, as the luminous red sun shimmered to a sliver on the horizon, I stood on the sixth floor balcony with John comfortably seated facing me, feeling the tropical trade winds massage my bare shoulders.

"Am I worthy of this?" I asked myself. Looking back at John, I gaped in marvel at a man who actually lived in this paradise.

"I cannot think of any place I would rather be than in Obama's hometown for Martin Luther King weekend." I inhaled the power of our sensible president and felt his fatherly glow. "You know, I actually met him once as a teenager when I'd vacationed here as a girl. He told me then that his name was Barry . . . adopted from his mother's pet name for him 'little bear'."

"I hate that fucker," he sighed, and turned to look at the shore. "I am hoping we get the change we need with Trump."

The balcony began to spin and I thought for an instant that the railing was going to detach from the side of the Aston and I would fall onto the street below. *Oh my God! Had this been something I'd forgotten to discuss? Could I be in the presence of Mortgage Broker in disguise? Maybe Mike could overlook such a thing, but I posolutely could not.*

I could have been more tactful. I could have used this opportunity to have a clear conversation with this beautiful man. Yet it was just weeks before the inauguration of Trump, signifying the end of a what-was-as-close-to-a-peaceful nation as we'd seen in generations.

My jaw set, I stumbled through the sliding glass threshold into the room. Steadying myself on the desk with the complimentary Aston Hotel notepad beaming my scrawl: dinner at the Duke, sunset cruise. My platforms buckled my ankles, causing me to fall onto the bed.

"You're going to have to leave, John," I choked, pointing at the door.

Bewildered, as if a vote for Trump was as natural as selecting a peach at the market, he spoke. "America needs some real changes and I agree we need to drain the swamp."

I examined John's perfect face and lips and begged my heart to pretend it didn't matter. Making love to pretty can be so pretty. Yet when I reached for the attraction that had pulled me so intensely across the ocean, the lustful glow was gone. His previous magnetism and my draw to it were completely undetectable. Here, I thought, was a boundary. A real hard-line wall that I could not ignore. I could not love this man, could not envision locking step with him. There was no way to camouflage it.

Picking up his coat and keys, John looked at me one last time with a "you crazy bitch" expression that solidified the thud with no chance of reconsideration.

Thank God.

The door closed slowly, due to today's hardware technology, which felt somehow soothing. I couldn't handle another slam at this point. I slumped heavily on my hotel room bed and pondered the impetuous decision I had made. Four days left in Paradise, and I had thrown out my handsome plans.

My sister in Seattle had Christmas-gifted me an expensive series of podcasts from a couple in the East Bay who taught classes and preached on

"Finding Your Soul Mate" via a "Love Breakthrough" workshop. I'd not opened the email with the podcast attachment for nearly a month.

"I don't need that shit," I had told her.

"But I love you and I want this for you," she had implored, with tears in her eyes.

My sweet older sister had always wanted the best for me. She often waited weeks to hear from me, like a patient parent. She knew what was best for me and supported my careening heart with a long, but solid tether. Here I was in sunny Hawaii, alone, with nothing else to do, and I thought, "what the hell, if it will make my sister happy."

The following morning, I spread out my blanket on the beach, pulled out my journal, and installed my ear plugs. Then, the podcast began. Lara and Johnny crooned, "Now find a quiet place to think and close your eyes, open your heart, and take a deep breath. Imagine you are in a peaceful place, like a beach." *Check.*

"Now take some time to write about the last year of your life, every detail." Clicking on the pause button, I texted Scoundrel. I wanted to start at the beginning.

> What did we do for New Year's last year?

> We did Tom Petty at the Greek Theater. Why?

I wrote for what felt like an hour, covering everything I could remember from working on the house to the mess I'd been left with after Europe. The tears were a deluge, like the rains back home.

"Now," Lara asked over my headphones, "what were you thinking?"

I stopped, set my pen down, and lay back. The sand was a warm, welcoming comfort. Two nearby children were fighting over what appeared to be real estate rights to a moat they'd constructed. I began to laugh loudly, rolling around like a puppy, causing them to look up and gaze at me.

This woman was a prophet.

Very similar to the practices of *The Artist's Way*, a book I'd just happened to have brought on this trip, Johnny and Lara assigned a series of practices. Be gentle with yourself, surround yourself with flowers. Sing, dance, go on an art field trip every week. And most important were the morning pages—one must write every day. I understood these things. Sister and I were both aware and talked frequently about our luck with having been raised in an artful family, with a mother who fostered love of craft and ritual. "Stay open to light, you are worthy of glowing." I listened, over the course of several mornings to this gentle guide, and was reminded, as I'd been reminded in Ireland, that my heart would remain open on this journey, bravery being my ballast.

I ruminated about John and how impulsively I had come so far to visit someone I didn't know at all. Should I call and apologize? What would I say? "I'm sorry you voted for Trump. I still want to be near you." That would be an untruth. Funny how a crush can fizzle, gone like water in a hot pan of grease.

Honolulu is a lovely island city. Not having been there since high school—a trip I'd taken with my old chum, Dani—as a grown woman I was intrigued with the history of the island. The Victorians that had crashed into native land contributed to a fascinating mix of cultures with the islanders. Nowadays, much of the town was covered with tony *Dubai-ish* shops like Vivienne Westwood and Gucci, clamoring for the young and wealthy Japanese visitors, all with surgically crafted faces and credit card eyes.

When Dani and I had been here thirty-five years ago, we'd stayed with a wealthy friend, Kelly, whose father's place was situated high in the Ilikai. We had partied many times with a skinny, biracial boy named Barry, and dated men who lived on boats, and washed our hair with hoses. We were reckless, then. Now, after nearly thirty years of being continuously in either a marriage or a relationship, why could I not drink from that carefree fountain again, ride my impulses like the Hawaiian surf and see what was ahead?

I packed up my towel and looked up two things on my phone—one: nearest botanical garden, two: OkCupid Honolulu.

The bus ride to the Foster Botanical Garden was ludicrously long, as it stopped every two blocks, but I used the time to acquaint myself with the people around me. Two young students, one from the Midwest with her French foreign exchange partner and an elderly Republican couple from Southern California with high, stiff, cottony hair, the male partner explaining to me his job of diverting tributary waters from spawning salmon. A colorful local whose native Hawaiian family had been here before Statesiders had encroached, was on her way to her job at Neiman Marcus.

When I finally lowered myself off the bus, looking for the entrance to the garden, I stumbled upon a huge, golden Buddhist temple, steaming with incense. The smoke serpentined through me with a heavenly antique fragrance of assurance—woody, musky, and earthy. I closed my eyes and opened my heart for a long, olfactory drink.

"If you could have anything in the world," whispered my heart. I entered the humid, sacred silence and allowed myself to feel small and grateful as I visually feasted on heaps of fruit and flowers thanking the light beyond. I was overwhelmed with the joy of being alone, a feeling I did not expect to have, ever. Silently creeping into the presence of God, I sensed something leading me from one emerging allegory to the next, and then, into the garden.

Foster, for which the botanical gardens were named, was most probably a Victorian curator wearing round spectacles with extensive knowledge of subtropical flora. Here, I met species I was unfamiliar with, like black pepper and bay rums, a world of bromeliads, orchids, and the talipot palm. As I was drinking in the Monarch-drenched frenzy in the Asclepias grove, I looked down, and there, on the ground, was a tiny, abandoned bird's nest, which I tucked into my purse. A sign, it seemed, of a safe home in my future. I didn't know yet where I was to live upon my return to the States.

I opted to call an Uber to return to my hotel. The Uber driver, Wendy, was a native to the island. When she arrived to pick me up on my corner, I slipped in beside her, rather than into the back seat, feeling loquacious. I told her of my experience at the gardens and she told me about her family. When we drove by the Ilikai Hotel and harbor, I asked if perhaps she could stop and let me look around.

Here in the harbor on a thirty-five-foot ketch with a killer spinnaker, I recalled aloud how, on my high school trip here, I had shacked up with a guy named Jim Morse. I was barely eighteen and he was thirty. I can't remember what I told my parents, though I had stayed two weeks with him on his boat. After I returned to California, his crush had lingered and he sailed his rig to Sausalito to visit me. But my feelings for him had faded by then, along with my tan.

"We're going to find him!" Wendy exalted, as she drove by every slip in the harbor. The thought that the guy would still be here forty years later was ludicrous, but she was caught in the adventure.

"Is that him? How about him? It's a love story, and I'm here to witness it!" We played out the folly for a while, then eventually I asked her to let me out to walk the beach back to the hotel along the shore, so I could languidly take in the day, the warm, salty water lapping up and kissing my knees. The following morning, I saw via my Uber app that Wendy had charged me just four dollars for the whole adventure.

OkCupid Honolulu offered up a few interesting dates. An ocean-tossed blonde with the dating title "Cowabunga" drove down the coast to teach me to surf one afternoon. We had no chemistry and he was far too young for me, but it was hilarious to learn of the surf culture and take out some *sick waves* with my new *brah*. I could barely keep up with this little Robinson Crusoe with his skin as tanned as a football. The next morning, I could barely move my legs.

I was slightly disgruntled that the fireman never showed up, after texting me very specific directions to an off-the-path bar. I walked for nearly a mile, through banyans and palms, my flip-flops caked with sticky pod sap, only to find what seemed to be some dude's backyard, devoid of any cute fireman.

I don't remember what Scott's OkCupid handle was; I wish I did. A funny, comfortable gentleman. He worked for the department of the interior, managing cultural park services and World War II Valor in the Pacific National Monument. When I learned that he oversaw all the diving on the USS Arizona, Utah, and Missouri in Pearl Harbor, I was impressed by his casual regard for a job that I found utterly fascinating. He picked me up in a car held together by gaffer's tape and bailing wire, explaining that he didn't give a shit about cars. Armed with turkey sandwiches and two beers, we pulled over on the south end of the highway. There, we slid down a steep, sandy cliff to a sunny beach.

I thought about home, where it was still pouring freezing rain, as I took off my shorts and blouse to expose the plunging swimsuit Mike had bought me. For Scoundrel, all swimwear, T-shirts, blouses, even sweaters for that matter, had to be plunging, thus he ordered them for me from tawdry catalogues. "Greatest tits!" he would say with a growl when I'd wear something he had bought for me.

Before Scoundrel, I had no idea the power I wielded between my shoulders. Breasts were a tool to feed infants and to carefully guard with sunscreen. When going out to win a client or present myself before a judge, Mike would inevitably spew a text, "Cleavage, baby!!!" always followed by several exclamation points.

As inappropriately sexist as Scoundrel was (is), in this case, I thought of his point as Scott politely blushed. From a netted bag, he pulled four fins, two masks, and snorkels. I thought it was sweet that he held my hand and gently guided me as we swam out in the rocky bay. I'm a strong swimmer, but an ocean is, after all, one of the Earth's forces, and there I felt small. This guy was obviously a merman at navigating current. We swam over to a cement piling where we admired the mansion of Doris Duke, a wealthy tobacco baroness, socialite, and philanthropist from the fifties. He must have actually read my profile and gleaned that I was captivated with history.

"I've secured a grant for a project in L.A. this summer to excavate the sunken World War II plane piloted by Gertrude Thompkins," he said, tearing off a chunk of his sandwich. "Would you like to come and assist?"

"Oh my God, that sounds fascinating! What would I do, photograph? I haven't gone scuba diving in years. It might be frightening."

"You can just be eye candy," he grinned, indicating my décolletage.

Checking my expression for offense, I flashed a kitteny smile to assure him the comment was endearing. I knew, having spent the day with him, that we were intellectual contemporaries, and quite honestly, with the exception of the Scoundrel, I find sexual compliments to come down the pike far too infrequently. It felt nice to be prized.

"I like that you let me flirt with you and not get your panties in a wad," Scott said, lowering his chin and looking up at me subserviently.

"You know, Scott, I can decide if I don't want to be spoken to like that. I think I have the freedom to say, 'buzz off, in your dreams, nice try' or simply 'no way, dude.' In this case, I find it refreshing to be attractive to you. I honestly don't know why so many women feel they haven't any power. We are, after all, animals. We have a dance. I wish more of my sisters could understand that they can decide to dance or sit. I honestly think we are scaring our men away. We may have dropped the ball on clear and responsible communication about consent and honest communication."

With that, Scott set down his sandwich, took my beer from my hand, and secured it with a twist in the sand. He pulled me up to a standing position. Placing his hand on my waist, he cupped my right hand and lifted it tenderly. Bringing his face six inches from mine, he looked dreamily into my eyes, and began to lead me in a perfect foxtrot.

We danced there on the beach for a good five minutes, ending with a bow and a curtsy. Laughing, I looked into his eyes, waiting for a kiss that did not come. I suppose he was waiting for me to make the overture. Perhaps I should have.

I flew back to the States with my *Quotations of Franklin D. Roosevelt* book on my lap from the World War II memorial that Scott had toured me through so comprehensively. I would see Scott one more time when he was passing through San Francisco. We met at the airport for a meal during a layover. His deep-sea excavation was postponed due to a terrible injury he'd incurred on some other risky reconnaissance. Months later, he texted me a picture of a lovely woman.

> My new girlfriend. We're coming to California for the weekend. Might you be into a threesome?

> In your dreams.

Coming home, whatever that was to be, was unavoidable. At least my daughter was curbside, waiting to hear of my trip.

"How'd it go with your handsome John?" She opened her car door from the inside to avoid the rain.

"He voted for Trump."

"Oh."

Home now, to rain and politics. I wished I could just hitch up to those living in paradise, rooting for the justice obviously masquerading as "just us." The starkness was just too clear, and so wrong.

In January, Trump, now in office, continued to push his promise to build a wall between the US and Mexico, insisting the Mexican government pay for construction. He suspended the Refugee Admissions Program and denied entry to citizens of Iraq, Iran, Libya, Somalia, Sudan, Syria, and Yemen as part of a Muslim ban. FBI director James Comey was invited to a one-on-one dinner with the President, where he was asked point-blank to pledge his loyalty. Trump appointed Steve Bannon as his chief strategist and we quietly watched in amazement as he passed a bill approving the Dakota pipeline and in turn the destruction of native lands. It was impossible not to feel hopeless. Yet, there was some light.

The day following Trump's inauguration, four million beautiful people around the world, including me, came together and peacefully demonstrated in the Women's March. This sea of love and an ocean of pink-pussy hats charged the world with power and elation. I felt so aligned with like minds, and even more inspired to celebrate my *she-ness*. I believe I grew a full inch that day.

As Soft as a Horse's Muzzle

Does every woman remember the first time she encountered a penis?

As far as I knew, my father didn't have a penis. He did have indecent, off-white Fruit of the Looms that rose up to his waist and sagged softly at the butt. My mother always smiled when the family got exposed to Dad's tighty-whities, which was rare. Her secret, behind-closed-doors fondness for him would flash before the shocked audience of my sister and me. I think I was fourteen when Mom was working through an argument with Dad and blindsided him with, "Well, one thing to be thankful for—we never have any trouble in the bedroom."

Wonderful Mom.

My brother had a penis, for sure, and I know that because when I was six and he was twelve, he contracted the fiercest case of poison oak rash in the world. This knowledge was augmented by the fact that his rash was everywhere. He sat in Aveeno oatmeal baths for days, wherein mother would emerge from the bathroom with an expression one might wear after enduring a freak show, the freak being her own offspring.

This region is sensitive, I gleaned from mishaps on the playground.

"Kick him in the balls!" my friends would shout. "What were balls?" I wondered, and why, if this was a well-protected area for boys, would we want to injure it? Sure, there was the Encyclopedia Britannica plastic peel-on-and-off pages of the human body that illustrated the extra piece on the man, yet it was just too odd to fathom, and best left alone.

When summering in Seattle with Grandma and Grandpa, we loved digging for clams at Great Aunt Stella's house in Gig Harbor. After begging mother to let me keep one of these giant mollusks, she offered up a coffee can of salt water and allowed me to place it bedside as a pet. I awoke in the night to witness the giant Geoduck member in full bloom and fingering over the rim of the Maxwell House can.

"It looks exactly like a penis!" my sister squealed when my scream brought her into my room.

Oh, God, what did she know that I didn't? I touched its velvet skin and it rippled and retracted. Soft and hypersensitive.

By the time I was eleven, I felt ready to learn more about this penis thing. Gina and Teresa Padilla, twins in a luscious Latino family boasting at least ten siblings, had a book. A dog-eared paperback entitled *Wet for Porn* was kept under Gina's mattress.

A group of six of us enjoyed telling our folks on summer nights that we were staying over at one another's house to make a slumber foray into the field. The field was an empty lot in our suburban subdivision, large enough that no one noticed our circle of sleeping bags around a makeshift campfire. This field was where we'd learned to climb rocks and trees, where we tore our clothes and challenged our courage, both physically and emotionally. There were so many big-eyed things unfamiliar and compelling about this crazy freedom. Grownups didn't know where we were. We were independent. Stoking our boundless fire, we shared our thoughts about possible boyfriends, the trending fashion of moccasins and Ditto jeans, and, most importantly, what kind of danger we could stir up. The uncomfortable twigs, cold winds, and uneven ground only made the experience more exotic. The sex book, which we pulled out late, was strangely provocative. Here, by flashlight, the penis was called a cock and its urgency to do taboo things was impossible not to read.

It was nasty.

He put his throbbing cock into her.

I burrowed into my sleeping bag, bringing my pillow in tight. "It throbs? This is horrible! Why would anyone want to do this? I am absolutely sure my parents do not do this."

"I don't know about the throbbing," Gina said, "but I do know my parents do it. I can hear them from our room, and how else can you explain why there are so many Padillas in our house."

"What does it sound like?" Kim asked.

Kim was my bestie and has remained so for life. We were inseparable. I knew her parents as well as my own. Roger and LaVera for sure did not have sex either, or one of us would have heard it.

"Keep reading, Gina!" Kim squealed, rolling over, eyes rolled back in a hysteria of laughter.

"*Shhhh*, not so loud," I whispered. "Yes, Gina, go on!"

The antics in this book of tawdry fiction were not designed for prepubescent girls still attached to their Girl Scout oaths and stuffed animals, but for more advanced pubescents. Yet, we kept reading, shouting out and laughing at the absurdity of it all, thus increasing our curiosity. We vowed to share with one another any and all information down the road that might demystify the confounding puzzle.

Our elementary school timed an introduction to sex with a series of films set up to explain that soon our bodies would be changing. Hair would suddenly appear under our arms and betwixt our legs and soon it would be necessary to say *no* to advances, lest we be shunned by our peers. "Prayer is not a reliable method" was the message. I had dreams of giant, throbbing penises marching at me in the night, with sports announcers echoing a warning of some pending peril over which I had no control. If sex was some kind of secret to keep from children, it must be worthwhile.

Two years later, I was receiving a lesson in diapering a child who was around the age of one. I was a mother's helper to a neighbor deeply in over her head with three youngsters. This was to be one of my duties. Holding the little boy's ankles with one hand, she lifted him effortlessly into the air so as to access his entire rump. Then with a warm washcloth she wiped his bottom and front region.

"You need to get into all those little folds" she demonstrated, gently nodding at his little button.

Well, hello penis! I wanted to throw my head back and laugh.

Not offensive or throbbing or disgusting by any stretch. Of course, it was fine. I felt delighted to add this new member to my vocabulary with such a quaint *kachink*. It looked soft and friendly, and when taking my turn at the chore, indeed it was.

The mother and I locked eyes and she smiled tenderly, not unlike my own mother's smile, which always imparted, "I love being here for this learning moment with you."

Fast forward to age sixteen, 1978.

Something about Monte Maroon moved me.

Although my family had moved across the reservoir to Orinda three years earlier, I still had close bonds with my childhood girlfriends ten miles away. Now, with a driver's license and my sister's hand-me-down Chevy Camaro, I could return to my old haunt and attend parties on weekends.

"I don't want you driving across the reservoir at night," my father would warn. "Too many deer trying to cross the road. You'll hit one and total your car."

"I'll stay with Kim and see you Sunday morning at church" always worked perfectly.

Yet, one Saturday night, I limped home after midnight, needing to be close to my parents after a perplexing episode.

We were in the converted basement of Gina and Teresa's after a cold and wet high school football game. Aside from my car, this party destination had the best collection of eight-track tapes and someone had managed to buy several cases of Michelob. Word had gotten out that when the boys had cleaned up after the game, they would join us.

The same six of us traversing life together for a decade were speculating on how many bottles of beer we could drink and still remember the words to our current favorite song, "Paradise by the Dashboard Light."

"I wonder if Monte will come?" Kim said, smiling at me, her eyes darting left and right. She had noticed me bristling when the two of us happened to be in the same universe. Monte was not particularly mature. Gangly and awkward, he was too tall for his age and his comely baby face was just showing signs of downy fuzz around his mouth. But that mouth. I couldn't explain my longing to kiss it, or at the very least, smell it. Monte was Latino, with caramel-colored shoulders and soft, brown, unkempt curls that tumbled down his face just below the jaw. He moved like a stallion, black mane in motion. I couldn't keep my eyes off him when he entered my frame of vision.

We had met weeks prior at Young Life, a supposedly Christian gathering of teens. One of the few places kids could assemble within the legal constraints of parents, and one reason my folks let me drive back to our old neighborhood. And drive back I did, most weekends, always hoping to get another glimpse of Monte Maroon. I hoped that he felt the same way.

It was nearing ten o'clock, the time Gina's parents had told us was to be curfew, when we heard the loud growl and screeching stop of a Ford Mustang in front of the house. This would be David White, Kim's love interest. We didn't have to strain to hear several male voices, all the age of our attraction.

My heart soared as I raced to the bathroom. Opening all the drawers at once, I found a brush full of a thousand children's hairs and used it to smooth my own, as well as some Bonnie Bell lip balm, Dr. Pepper-flavored. The sweet taste and gentle color it gave my lips was so rewarding that I pocketed the treasure.

The boys came in through the side door that entered straight into the basement. There were more than six of them, and I wondered how they had all fit into one car. They were as drunk as I'd ever seen anyone, including the hobos on television. It was endearing how helpless Monte seemed as he fell in a heap onto Gina's lime-green beanbag chair. I sat down on the floor beside him and folded my knees in tight enough to pull my sweater over them to warm myself.

"Good game," I lied. I knew nothing about football, and although attending high school games was something we did, we never actually watched. Sporting events were a place where we took stock of who was there, and if our peers had any idea of what we were supposed to be doing. We scrutinized one another's antics and reactions, fumbling to understand where we fit into the tribe. My hair was particularly soft that evening as the misty air gave it a riverlike body.

"Come here." Monte pulled my wrist, causing me to land on his lap. He was bigger than I was by a long shot, and for some reason, I felt safe in his lap. Without hesitation, he pulled my jaw into a long, wet kiss. I had kissed a boy before, but not like this. His tongue probed the inside of my mouth as if it were searching for something to consume.

What happened next was blurry. Something about standing and kissing, leaning up against a wall and kissing, then like a dream, we were on a sofa alone. Unbuckling his belt and lowering his jeans, we struggled to get his pants past his hips then off a leg in the dark.

"Okay," I thought, "where is this thing?"

Traversing my hand up his thigh I found it. An iron rod in a velvety encasement. Cartilage covered by the softest skin I've ever felt. Like a horse's muzzle.

"I've never done this," he whispered. "Are you alright?"

Was I alright?

Instantly, I felt a waterfall of tenderness toward this boy. My only desire was my desire to understand desire, yet I could appreciate his desperation. I supposed it was my role to act as if I were as ravenous as he.

Was I alright?

"Yes," I breathed into his neck. His bouquet of Zest soap, cheap beer, and Wrigley's Doublemint gum would be one I would not forget.

I searched my soul for lust, but what I landed on was camaraderie. I was doing this boy a favor, and he, I. His body was soft, precious, wide, and warm. I glimpsed into his yearning heart and reveled in the closeness. What an honor to be the beneficiary of human reciprocity.

There was some pushing, some panting, some hot breath in my ear. His eyes rolled back into his soft black curls, then, after a long sigh, he fell asleep. He was pretty, I remember that. A boy, just my age, who was morphing into a man. Sinewy muscles of a young warrior craving a hunt. Running my fingers down his hairless chest, I bent in to smell this new flesh that I'd found, then turned my head to rest there. The connection was sweet and entirely new.

I returned to our home in Orinda late and brushed my teeth, washed my face, put on a T-shirt, and turned out the lights. Remembering that my folks liked to know when I was home, I groped down the long dark hall to Mom and Dad's room and cracked open the door.

"I'm home."

"Well, thank goodness" was always mother's response. Yet, this time she added clairvoyantly, "Are you alright?"

I longed to climb in next to her and wrap myself in her gigantic bosom, to tell her what had happened, and that yes, I was all right, and wildly curious about what sex meant. I yearned for her pearls of wisdom to smooth out my questions. I wanted to be close to my mother as I'd crossed this chasm from virginity to womanhood. I'd somehow fumbled through an important ritual without the warmth of her guidance. I hadn't known I could do that.

In hindsight, I wish I had crawled in next to her, but sixteen-year-olds don't do that.

The Grace of The Goddess

By the time February 2017 rolled in, the female energy around the world was electrically unified. Feeling completely luminous and porous, I was a walking instrument of symbiosis. Since the Women's March, there was a new dynamic infiltrating all of my sisters. A visceral buoyancy permeated us all. Sparks flew when female eyes met. My spiritual high was a buzz that replaced my longstanding fear of scarcity, heights, and freeways.

While enjoying tea with a friend in the village, a phone call came in requesting "a headshot right now." This kind of thing never happened. Generally, photography sessions of any sort are set up at least a week in advance. She let me know that she was comfortable doing her own hair and makeup, and we agreed to meet at my studio in twenty minutes.

Theresa was light and airy, with sapphire eyes and a glorious mane of black hair curling down her back. I always chat as I shoot clients to help them feel comfortable, and was attempting to explain my feelings about the march and sisterhood.

"I can't really put my finger on it," I confided, "maybe it is all this dating I'm doing. Our collective power feels so electric."

"You are right about this rise of feminine power. You know, I am not only a therapist, I am also a priestess."

Well, of course she was . . . and she was put in my path for some supernatural reason, as were Rose and Mary in Dublin.

"I feel pretty sure we've captured several good shots." I spoke candidly now. "Would you mind if I turn on the fan and have some fun?"

The images from the session were prismatic. Sure, I do a damn good headshot, but these were special. Looking at them, the feminine power was unmistakable. Before me was a supernatural, eternal woman. Her eyes extolled a timeless wisdom. Her hair a shimmering blaze of fire, a story that begged to be told.

I asked Theresa if I could use one of her images to launch a new idea. A photojournalistic piece, "The Goddess Project." Here I would actively search out women of political and social change, dress them like Warrior Goddesses holding an object of power, then write about each one. For this journey, I knew that I would need to say *yes* to any and all divining rods placed in my path surrounding the subject.

Morphing my daily wardrobe to include huge leather belts and gemstones, I felt power. After the fall from the Hawaii affair, I dove into the solace and steady platform developing from surrounding myself with intelligent women of change.

Like an emancipated Victorian, I wanted to get involved in everything feminine and powerful. I did a Facebook search for groups that featured women activists and found several groups that advertised events. With one simple click on "Going," my calendar was filled.

These events, in tandem with my active dating life, transformed me into a colorful socialite. I wanted to meet people who were doing things, influencing, and making things move, as well as the everyday mothers on the front lines. I formed an exhilarating model of my vision and cast my luminous net wide.

First stop, the online network of my neighbors. I posted a shout-out on Nextdoor.com. "Who here is a Goddess?"

I received a response from Emily, a beautiful young woman with tawny hair down to her waist, perfectly cared-for nails, and a heart as wide as the prairie.

"We," she vamped, "have been through hell and back and could sure use some celebration."

She was referring to herself and two other close friends, accompanied by a collection of daughters, one identifying as trans. After I explained to her that I'd like to photograph each woman individually and then together as a group, she wanted to know where I was aiming my message.

"We have a president in office who believes it's acceptable to grab a woman by the pussy."

"It's fucking surreal," she smarted.

"Remember how the Women's March felt? I want to highlight our power as women. I want to show both our strength and our spirit. Think invincible, think Goddess, think supernatural."

"I've got it!" she trumpeted. "Please let me style."

The next week, Emily showed up at my studio with dozens of flowy dresses, headdresses, gems, candles, and necklaces. We lovingly dressed these important women, preening and anointing the strength and individuality of each, then turned on the fan for effect while the creative serotonin guided my lens.

I decided to work on postproduction on my laptop sitting in Mountain View Cemetery, since I know so many energizing souls there. Leaning up against Chloe Buckel's headstone (the first woman doctor in Oakland), I edited and decided on the feeling and tone of this photo story.

When I finally reviewed what I'd put up, I figured I'd outdone myself; it was like tasting last spring's strawberries in autumn's jar. I felt alive as I drove around and around the decorative water fountains of Olmstead's funeral gardens, blasting tribal music from my car. I saw a beam of light glimmer through one of the fountains, as though something celestial had touched down.

This photographing of women, I thought, was something I could do to celebrate the goodness of our people, in contrast to all the dismantling going on. It was no accident that this work was an embrace of the feminine in the context of the most toxic aspect of the masculine.

In February 2017, *The New York Times* was barred from the White House press briefing room, along with the BBC, CNN, *The Los Angeles Times*, and

The Huffington Post. President Trump proposed a ten-percent, fifty-four-billion-dollar increase in military spending diverted from numerous other budgets, including that of the State Department and the Environmental Protection Agency. Congress received a letter criticizing this plan. It was signed by more than a hundred and twenty retired US admirals and generals, including a former army chief of staff George Casey Jr.

President Trump acknowledged that he paid a hundred and thirty thousand dollars to adult film star Stormy Daniels as hush money for an alleged extramarital affair. *The New York Times* reported that Trump had a nine-month extramarital affair with *Playboy* model Karen McDougal, citing handwritten documents from Ms. McDougal. Tom Shannon, the US Secretary of State for Political Affairs, announced that he would be resigning for personal reasons.

Were these the changes John had been referring to during my intrepid trip to Hawaii?

The Drama Farm

Hell-bent on staying in the Oakland Hills, I found a master bedroom for rent in a house just up the street from Scoundrel's. It turned out to be the home of a fix-it man who'd done a lot of work for me in the remodeling of Mike's house. I was surprised to learn that Warren Fix-it-Man actually owned such a nice place, after assuming his income was meager.

A single guy with part-time custody of his thirteen-year-old girl, Warren and his daughter, Sashy, lived downstairs in a huge, converted living room, complete with a river rock fireplace. Upstairs was me in the master bedroom adjacent to another renter, Molly, with whom I shared a bathroom. Molly was a spellbinding artist of every medium who made her living fabricating prosthetic limbs.

Right before my move, Mike had made me custodian of his house and dog, while he and Mortgage Broker vacationed in Sayulita, Mexico, which happened to be our former, favorite annual love nest.

Scoundrel and I had opted to continue our split amicably. There was just far too much entwined to untangle. We shared a studio, he leased my car and paid for my medical insurance and the country club, which could never know we weren't married or my abs of steel would soften, loosening my toe-hold in the marketplace of love. He hadn't minded me living with him and sleeping in his bed, but the new girl wanted exclusive rights to my former boyfriend, so we'd been platonic since the fallout.

The day before my move to Warren's, I went into the woods in the early morning with Meadow and Ricky, my dogs and Scoundrel's. Then I sat with a thick stack of blank paper at our favorite picnic table, where we had played Scrabble on balmy summer nights. Covering a good five or six pages with a black felt tip pen, I wrote down everything I could remember from the last five years. Meeting Mike in the bar, him proclaiming that he was the mayor of Montclair, me producing the book of photographs I had published on the same village where we had both raised kids of the same age for well over twenty years. How could we have both known so much about this community but never have known each other? Meeting for a walk and realizing both our dogs had the same markings. The dizzy falling in love, holding hands while we slept. His words, "I love going to parties with you because the prettiest girl in the room is mine." Saving me from losing the house by moving me in with him and renting mine out to filmmakers. The remodel . . . how we'd used a camp sink on the deck for weeks, raccoons marauding our supplies. The extensive travel, the cabin in Tahoe. All the clothing he bought me so I would always be sexy. Mike was the first man I'd dated who was nearly shorter than I was. We were like children together, audibly farting for a laugh. He would text me pictures of his boner, waiting for me to return from my hikes. I would miss this man-cub, who'd never lost his keys or been more than one minute late for anything. I would miss his relentless attention and our ever-flowing, glamourous plans, his perfect teeth flashing at me as he'd change his clothes for dinner. All of this aside, I would not miss his temper. Dodging his rage had reduced me. Because the relationship was not a fit, everything was as it should be.

I called the consignment store and found a dining room table for Scoundrel's house to replace my mother's table that I'd be taking along with me; I had it delivered. I would also be taking my sofa and king-sized bed, replacing them for Mike with those Warren was ready to cast off.

To help with the move, I looked up the lovely man from Trinidad who owned a moving truck and had moved me previously. My family had named him "Joseph the Prophet" for his ability to make any move a pleasure.

Waiting among a pile of boxes, I collapsed on the bed that was to move with me and allowed myself to rest and ponder my future. The bedroom I'd shared with Mike was not designed to be a bedroom, but a downstairs rumpus room with a parquet floor and sliding glass door, which I slid open to listen to the gentle wind of the late morning. Just 10:00 a.m., and I was already weary from loneliness and insecurity.

I thought about Mike, probably riding an ATV down the long cobblestone driveway in our familiar spring vacation spot—a Mexican fishing village—legs sprawled high in front of him, his new girlfriend straddling and chirping, holding his waist tightly. There was nothing I could do to be the object of his frivolity again, nor would it be right. Yet the ludicrous ease of his life in contrast with the perilous reality of my own was a palpable problem, now my business with a capital "B." Not a problem solved by anything but my own determination to find my own way.

Rereading the lengthy letter I had scrawled, I let it fall gently on the nightstand, setting his reading glasses atop it. I could hear Joseph the Prophet backing into the driveway. The old U-Haul truck he had repainted, removing the "U" and adding "*ing*," followed by his cell phone number. I recognized the sigh and screech of the heft against the brakes.

"Hello, sister. You ready for an adventure?" Joseph showed up in times of transition with a malty Caribbean comfort.

Alongside a delicious British diction, his arms were big and capable, his dewy chocolate skin impervious to weakness or doubt. When he laughed, I wished I could bottle the sound and keep it close to me. I wondered if a female recipient of this treasure was out there somewhere, and if she knew how lucky she was.

"May I present my partner, Ryan." Joseph had a different partner every time he worked, most likely someone he had picked up from the labor pool corner near the downtown train station.

Ryan was wiry and disheveled, down on his luck for whatever had caused him to look so unwell.

My dog Rick and I rode with Ryan and the Prophet in the tiny hub of the truck just ten houses up the street, to what would be later dubbed the "Drama Farm."

There, at Warren's house, I had a gentle breakdown. My heart racing from moving chaos, I was greeted by my new housemate, Molly, and little Sashy, Warren's thirteen-year-old, who busied themselves making my bed and setting up my mother's dining room table with cloths and candles. The sensation of entering a feminine Montessori, a collection of girls of assorted ages, was a rapturous comfort.

Out of nowhere came my tears. Relief, exhaustion, and gratitude let down like mother's milk in the proximity of her own infant.

"Why are you crying?" Sashy asked.

"Trauma," Molly interpreted, as she brought me a glass of coconut water and a boiled egg.

Slowly chipping off the fragmented shell into a bowl, she cut it in half, using her palm as a cutting board, salted and peppered it, and offered it up on her outstretched hand.

"We're glad you're here." She seemed at ease.

She was so young, early twenties, but something about her suggested she'd experienced a great deal.

After seemingly everything was unloaded from Joseph's truck, my Caribbean compatriot made one last trip to his vehicle and returned carrying a gift for us all. It was the nature of his trade to collect treasures that others had cast off.

The large rectangular glass aquarium was sizable, even in his arms, and I could make out a fake fern and faux resin rock formed into a water bowl. Clearing a space on our newly acquired kitchen table, Joseph reached into the tank and produced a juvenile African tortoise. As it wriggled its feet in midair, Sashy instinctively reached out with cupped hands to secure the creature's toes. It retreated immediately as she drew it to her face like it was a sandwich and she needed to determine its contents. Just then, Warren appeared from downstairs to survey the move-in.

"Dada, look!" Sashy said, beaming. "Can we keep him?"

Warren seemed pleased that I'd come with a pet beyond my dog.

"It's not mine" I explained. "Joseph, my mover, is offering him up. What do you think?"

I was charmed that Warren accepted the gesture without balking. My sister frequently mails me statuary, jewelry, and messages of turtles as totems of safety. This seemed an omen—a house on my back.

My room was even higher up the mountain than Scoundrel's house, thus the view was phenomenal, with a door to the deck that boasted a rocking chair overlooking the world. Unlike Scoundrel, who I used to wake up with the paper and a coffee at ten, these people at Warren's rose at 6:00 a.m. It was a warm and caring, multigenerational situation full of art, devoid of television. I would wake with the family, help send Sashy and Molly off to school and work, respectively, then rest back in bed to write or edit photo work.

Warren was a tech man who had let go of his career to spend more time with Sashy, and he took on jobs as a handyman seemingly because there was literally nothing he couldn't fix. He was forty-something, obsessed with growing things from seed, and always had a huge pile of "building materials" in his driveway because you never knew when something might be useful. He shopped at Costco frequently and kept us fed with an armory of supplies. I so enjoyed living with a young, strong man to whom I had no attachment other than to his exemplary provisional qualities: strength and capability.

Molly and I enjoyed each other immensely, going to museums and performances regularly. She was interested in my Goddess Project and loved hearing stories of the women I was enlisting, as well as about the men I was dating. We shared a bathroom with a good ceramic tub. She was young and stunning.

Subjected to a melee of rash decisions, her soft and dewy skin haphazardly displayed murals of hastily decided-on, yet permanent, tattoos, as if she'd attempted to veil her beauty. From her ankle to her thigh climbed an unfinished, demonic depiction of squirrels clutching a spooky tree. On her shoulder, a black jagged line like that seen on the screen of a life-support monitor intersected a human skull. She often concealed this body art with clothing. When she was in shorts and a tank top, though, it was like looking at the ocean floor during low tide, all flotsam and jetsam visible.

She would wake early, slither into her blue draw-string scrubs and beckon her Malamute, Ruby, to jump into her half-ton truck. Ruby, she had explained, was her service dog. "She keeps me sane." Which seemed like an easy excuse for allowing your pup to join you to work in a prosthetic limb fabrication mill.

Our time together was textural. There was literally nothing Molly couldn't draw, make, or craft. I brought her to the Oakland Museum's White Elephant Sale, where she bought yards of fur and leather to transform into amazing Burning Man headpieces. One evening, she pulled out an envelope filled with thousands of paper irises she had painstakingly cut out of flower catalogues, and together we lay them out to form a colossal Rorschach-like-image to be glued onto foam core.

"Over here, please." She waved her hands over an area of the canvas. "More of the purple to flow down here to the magenta. Back up. See? It's like a lava flow. See?"

Warren sat down to join us, blessing his own ideas of where the yellow petals might work. "I like bringing these lighter ones up here. What do you think, Moll?"

We watched her eyes pulse over the work, directing the production like we were a dance troupe. I could nearly hear gears spinning in her head as she pursued her color intuition. After an hour of working and reworking the piece, at last she said, "Yes, that's it. I feel its violence, don't you?"

Securing the glue with a parallel panel, we piled several books on top of our masterpiece to keep it flat while it dried. The following morning, I observed her standing over the piece. The glue had buckled and shriveled the paper petals. It was a loss. Worried about her letdown, I laid my hand on her shoulder.

"I love it because it represents the process, not the product, you know?" she said, as she carried it out to the recycling bin. "With this many irises, maybe the green bin?"

Molly had been raised on the road by her caring hippie parents. Her dad had been in the Peace Corps, but Molly seemed nonplussed by the disorder around her and would spend hours crafting. Her homemade lip scrubs and herbal face-mask activities with Sashy were important because they were with Sashy. She was diligent with her job, sometimes putting in thirteen-hour days, which seemed excessive to me. Occasionally, she seemed frightened, and I would fold her into my arms where I felt a dark fragility that I attempted to fortify with intentional love. Countless hours of milling prosthetics had calloused her palms and rendered them as rough as sandpaper. I felt her adrift; her harbor-grey eyes conveyed a call for oars.

Savant, I reasoned. I have occasionally encountered people with an island full of genius surrounded by an ocean of sensitivity. I longed to protect her and allow her some light to ferry her over her own mania.

My work got fairly steady during my time at the Drama Farm. Some kind of abundant miracle, the clients continued to call at just the right frequency. In the studio downtown, I photographed babies, families, lawyers, lovers, writers, and, occasionally, celebrities. Each day, as I would prepare to drive down to the shop, maneuvering coffee, laptop, packed lunch, my pup Rick, and camera equipment into the car—difficult due to the mounting garbage pile, I often heard Mike driving up the hill to bring his dog to the woods, Tom Petty's *Free Fallin'* Doppler-ing by.

Walter from the OkCupid site was eight years younger than me, but Dani assured me that you take your age, cut it in half and add seven, and you're still within your league. Men date younger women all the time, why on earth should it not work the other way?

I'd recently discovered I was better suited to being a cougar of sorts. When I was younger, I was not nearly as voracious a lover as I'd become in my fifties. Plainly speaking, I had no idea where my arms were supposed to go for the first decade of my sexual awareness. Highly self-conscious of my large breasts and blushing décolletage, I assented to sex being something done to me, not with me, let alone, *for me.* Acceptance was the goal in the spring of my life; pleasure came much later. It took me a universe of intimacy with solid partners to find what really felt like a stellar connection and dizzying pleasure. Men, I've intimated, have more of an appetite before their sixtieth birthday. After that, I've found them to behave much like an old dog, lifting their head only when a car drives by. I am not yet ready for hearing aids, arthritis, and erectile dysfunction. I'll do that with my best man-friend down the road.

Younger men are not without problems. Many are not substantial enough to hang your proverbial hat on, leaning on inexperienced words such as "totally" and "for sure." They can be embarrassing at parties and are frequently fresh out of a shitty marriage.

The latter was the case with Walt. Educated in New Orleans to be an architect in our chilly city of San Francisco, he had two very young children, which for me proved to be an asset. I love children, consider my time with them a great contribution, and could happily work myself into any situation to teach and learn from them. Yet Walt was suffering a gruesome divorce from an abusive, soon-to-be ex-wife. Without the financial freedom to pay for two homes, he was surfing a friend's couch and picking the kids up for his court-appointed custody time. Everything he did was aimed at stabilizing his babes, which I admired. Kid crossovers, during which he and his ex were forced to encounter each other, were excruciating. Sometimes Walt would text me from the bathroom, where he would stash himself until the arguments stopped and he could emancipate himself with the children.

Walt and I saw each other not nearly often enough for my taste. I would reach out every few months and invite him to a slumber party, which he would attend with his guitar. He played and sang beautifully. His black button-up shirt sent me to the moon, his eloquence and tenderness fit me like a glove. Lying next to him and his eyes of a thousand blue rivers, I would wonder out loud why he couldn't rest himself in my heart.

"Fear," he explained.

Though I felt certain I could not let go of all the wonders he was, we were simply in different universes. I vowed to keep him in my heart like a pebble of Almond Roca in my molar, dipping in for a taste whenever it was offered.

This was the man, I sensed, I could love forever. I opted for the love to live suspended without ties.

"I don't want to hurt you," he said, as if he knew that he would.

A situation of "let go and let live" was paramount here.

I learned from Walt, qualities that I admired, and tucked them into my suitcase-heart.

Hints for Ladies Who are Dating

Over time, I've devised a certain set of rules, routines, and realities for dating. Practical hints from experience that I think might serve us all. Have I always followed them? Well, this is, after all, a memoir, a string of pearls that didn't spill out all at once. But because by now in these pages I've established myself to be all-in on this love-lab experiment, I feel I've the acumen to share a few nuggets of wisdom.

Rule 1

It's fun to swipe right and left on a dating site, but I've found it time well spent to give a profile some study prior to hasty swiping. Learn what left versus right means, and understand how to get to the actual profile. At first glance, many boys love skiing and kiteboarding, read Michael Chabon, and are looking for that special someone with whom they can journey to the end of the world. Yet, the fine print is paramount. Do they appear to have the means to travel? Does this body look as if it has had any physical activity in recent decades? Don't overlook comments like "my wife thinks you're hot," or "my dog thinks you're hot." Shopping sprees used for retail therapy often end in superfluous baggage. The same applies when shopping for a mate. It's always awkward if you don't do your homework and find yourself face-to-face with a psychopath.

"They're here, too," Mother used to say when referring to the oddballs we share the planet with.

Rule 2

Ask his political bent up front. Period.

Rule 3

Plan your date with the discretion to gracefully bail. I generally opt for a short hike, coffee, or a cocktail. Coffee is an excellent starter. Bring a backgammon board. If he can remember the board setup and asks for a rematch, he could be worth a second look. Walking and talking is a nice way to review a new prospect, and if there's a dog with you, all the better. I always have a friend on the ready to call me on cue and say rather loudly into the phone, "Your place has been burgled. Come immediately!"

Rule 4

Regarding texting. A form of communicating that will last until my granddaughter's generation—over my dead body. This sloppy tool offering dopamine-driven cues can turn things quite topsy-turvy. Every texting mistake I have ever made was from misconstrued communication without eye contact, typos, or late-night drinking.

Should you decide to move from an online site to texting, don't spend more than four days dialoguing via text. Four is the absolute maximum before sitting face-to-face with your suitor (more on this later). Should you fancy someone after meeting him in person, which demonstrates that he is real, don't assume his inability to return texts indicates he's been in a fatal accident. This oversight merely reflects an atrophy of the frontal lobe that occurs in a surprisingly large number of dating men.

Equally important to heed . . . under no circumstances should you continue to badger a man who is not responding to your outreach. There is much to glean from the techniques of our foremothers in their corsets and gloves. Create some mystery by dropping your glove. If he doesn't pick up what you're putting out, move on.

Rule 5

Don't drive (or fly) too far and don't buy new clothes for a first date. Don't wear dumb shoes or pay for fancy up-dos, ever. You never know when you might need to climb out of a bathroom window, or God forbid, run. As learned in the book, *The Tao of Dating*, dress to the sevens, rather than the nines. Men don't care about clothes or shoes. They care about what makes them feel good. If he becomes the man with whom you wish to tarry, you can do it in flip-flops.

Rule 6

You are the only person focused on the lines on your face. "All that they see is your essence," my sister tells me. I'm going with that.

Rule 7

Committing to a dinner can be problematic and expensive, yet if you already like a gentleman who recommends one of your favorites, this could hurry the process of weeding out the non-check-picker-uppers. Yes, I am a feminist, yet I still cling to some traditional roles and mores. A man picking up the check and holding a door is, in my mind, not the sign of a chauvinist.

Rule 8

Follow your heart. Don't settle for someone because he is simply a plus-one for the Rotary picnic or a passing warm body. You risk hurting someone, and that, again, takes time and valuable heart space. When you see him, you'll know it and it won't have to do with looks.

Rule 9

Lean out. Try to continue to focus on the things that make you wonderful: your work, your hobbies, your art, and most importantly, your health. These qualities of yours are what will make you attractive.

Rule 10

Dance. As frequently and fervently as possible.

Rule 11

Never lie and you won't have to remember anything. Complete, bold honesty is fundamental in discovering who you are and where he fits. If what you are feels incongruent with what he is, keep swimming.

Rule 12

Keep your contacts straight. If you might want to see a contestant again, save his first and last name with a photo in your phone so as not to mix up your "Tims."

Rule 13

Don't be anxious; this is an adventure. You've nothing to lose and all to gain from meeting new people. Every person in your life adds dimension, whether you feel attraction to that person or not. I learned quickly the drill of preparation—what is easy to wear and what to have in my purse: breath mints, gardenia hand cream, lip liner and lipstick, powder, and a brush.

Rule 13 (a)

Attain the skills to apply all of these while driving.

Rule 14

Breathe in the dating experience with curiosity and wonder, rather than a sense of failure.

Rule 15

Write that shit down. Your daughter will find your dating exploits fascinating.

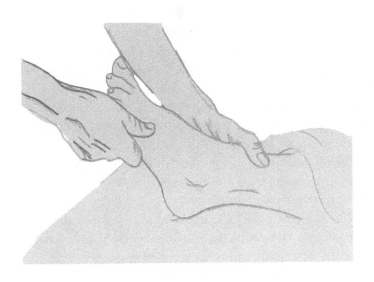

Tony-ssage

Isabella runs a salon not far from my studio. Her brilliant red lipstick always slightly askew, she's been known as the woman who can keep you laughing all the way through a Brazilian waxing. The sexiest sixty-five-year-old Latina you'd ever have the joy to know. Her place is all roses and Bette Midler music. She does skin care in her leggings and boots that rise high above her knees like a she-pirate's, while Maria, her partner, does hair. You can walk in any day and enter the world of *La-La*. Isabella might be embroidering while singing; Maria doing a permanent wave on an old gal of the village. Emoting the priestess energy of yesteryear, this is where you will inevitably find the community's celebrated ninety-one-year-old Loud Lady getting her nails done while ranting inappropriately about the Orientals taking over her block.

Isabella and I bartered photos for skin care. She made my brows express my mood and smoothed my face with steam and lavender. I, in return, brought her into the studio and flashed four-hundred frames of her making love to the camera like Marlene Dietrich.

Maria liked the trade idea as well and asked if I'd let her give my hair-do a try in exchange for some new promotional images.

Running her soothing polished fingertips across my scalp, she assessed what she was dealing with. I've always been generally underwhelmed with my hair. It won't grow past my shoulders and the mousey brown has been covered for years with countless boxes of L'Oreal 10A, extra-light ash blonde. Over time, it tends to fade to a brassy orange that's not right for my face. Maria seemed to understand this.

"What we need here," she bolstered, "are some warm lowlights and cool highlights, as well as a thirty-minute intensive conditioner. And let's try bangs." It was evident that she knew what she was doing. As she skill-fully fluttered a black smock over my chest and snapped it snuggly at the nape of my neck, I settled into my swively chair, deliciously anticipating time with a new friend that touches during talk.

"You hold these foils and hand them to me when I ask," she said, as she lay a box of individually folded rectangles of thin aluminum on my lap, "and tell me about you."

The back of her rat-tailed comb traced a line from my forehead to the nape of my neck as she picked up a small selection of hair strands. Then, using the comb to hold the folded foil under the tiny tress, she painted a white, ammonia-smelling paste over the top of the encapsulated hair and folded the edges to seal it tightly like a precious package. Flipping it over my head like a card in a rolodex, she effortlessly moved on to the next. This could take some time, I thought, as each sweep of her pencil-sharp rattail comb tingled my viscerally receptive scalp; I was like a cat leaning into a good scratch.

Hairdressers tend to nurture great relationships, probably because they are tenders of the body, as well as the heart. Like a primate mother gently picking bugs from her infant's scalp, a hairdresser offers time to listen, or if what you need is complete silence, she may allow you to choose that as well. I opted to dive in.

"Well, I'm dating," I said with an exhale. "Aggressively, since my boy-friend of five years started fucking a mortgage broker. I'm also working on a new coffee-table book about Goddesses."

I watched her intrigued expressions as I shared my exploits. All the while, I continued to pass her foils, my new silver mane transforming me into a galactic lion.

I hadn't noticed others in the salon milling about until Maria, needing access now to the back of my head, swung my chair ninety degrees left. There, in the chair neighboring mine, sat a most alluring young man.

Comfortably slumped in the neighboring salon chair, he rested his feet on the counter of blow dryers and curling wands, exposing tanned, sockless ankles over youthful Vans. I became acutely aware of how ridiculous I looked in my silver helmet.

"What constitutes a Goddess?" He smiled sarcastically, as if he already knew the answer.

He was simply drop-dead beautiful. Carved purely from the quarry of creation, his butterscotch skin was flawless and when he spoke his upper lip curled up intentionally like a hungry kitten. Parted in the middle, and deliberately too long, his blonde hair reminded me of the Great Gatsby's. He studied my answer as if testing me for accuracy.

"In short, a divine chick." I went into my elevator speech. "Women's role in society is as essential as a honeybee's, everybody knows that. So . . . with our government in shambles, celebrating our determined power is essential. The women I am highlighting in this photographic book are spiritual and political changemakers. I'm dressing them in regal, flowy garb with big leather belts and gigantic statement pieces. Each woman has an object that she brandishes. It's fun and powerful. I'm meeting some truly amazing gals on this quest and my stylist and I are like kids in a candy shop. What is your role here in Isabella's salon? Observer?"

"Pretty much." His body emoted an ease as if nowhere to go was enormously relevant. "I'm Tony. I offer massage and acupuncture in the back room here."

"Well, sign me up," I smirked.

The following week I came in for my first Tony Treatment. I boldly stripped off my clothes before he could say, "here's a drape, I'll be back in a moment." I was hoping to shock him.

He threw me an "I'm a doctor" expression and asked me to lay down on the table so he could adequately cover me with his pink sheet. "On your back first."

Running his hands over my sheeted body from crown to toe, he closed his eyes to sense what he was dealing with, then lifted my hand and held it firmly in his Swedish grip. My heart rose like the tide. Everything in this salon had come to be a delicious comfort, his nurturing being no exception.

His hand engrossed in mine, he lifted it high and began playing my forearm like a mandolin, gently reading my hidden stories. His eyes rolled back in his head. I prepared myself for bad news. Could he sense the isolation, the cigarettes, the thousands of losses surrounding me?

"Your liver is damp," he murmured, "but your Qi is super strong. Tell me what's going on in your life."

I told him that I'd been doing a trade with Isabella and Maria. "That's what brought me here. My photography studio is right upstairs."

He removed a tiny needle from its sterile wrapper and tapped it adeptly between my palm and thumb as he continued to speak. "How long have you been dating?"

"Jesus Christ!" I shrieked. "Could you give me some warning please?"

"*Shhhh!*" He laughed. "The salon gals will think there is something odd going on in here."

There was something odd going on in here.

As Tony skillfully speared each of my pressure points, I felt a whirling, blissful, electrical opiate sensation. My eyes felt cemented shut as I envisioned myself as Guliver, rendered useless by a thousand tiny archers, designing a plan to tie me to Tony's table.

Over time I became a slave to this addiction. A blatant dance of supernatural intensity aligning Tony's and my spiritual river with intelligence, clarity, honesty, and humor. Outside the particle-board door, the crowded salon would chirp, oblivious, Barbara Streisand and Enya running the soundtrack.

These treatments became a weekly ritual with Tony. I felt a deep satisfaction just from being near him and naked. With seemingly no regard for money, our sessions—sometimes acupuncture, sometimes massage, usually both—often lasted two hours, for which he would ask, "maybe forty bucks this time?"

What evolved was a lasting and nurturing friendship. While he would run his yummy fingers up and down my body, we would talk about everything from my work, my Goddess Project book, his dying father, our history, our ambitions, political incredulities, and our feelings about pretty much everything. Sometimes, in the midst of a caress, he would stop and open his laptop to share with me a song or YouTube piece. One afternoon, he narrated a poem by Rumi about a maidservant who had cleverly trained a donkey to perform the sexual services of a man.

From a gourd, she had carved a flanged device to fit on the donkey's penis, to keep him from going too far into her. She had fashioned it just to the point of her pleasure.

Good God, he made me laugh, but never once was there any way on earth that Tony would consider being my boyfriend. I outright asked him, to which he playfully slapped my sheet-shrouded bottom and stated, "I'm not attracted to you, Reen."

While on my back, I would stare into his Warren Beatty face, blonde curls tumbling across his velvet eyes. I'd watch his darling penny loafers without socks when I was belly down and pine to have a life with him. Yet this new fraternal demonstration of something deep and meaningful struck a profound chord in me. Had something romantic ever happened between us, I would not have my precious *Tony-ssage*, as I went on to call this sweet ritual.

"We are . . ." he assured me, leaning his upside-down eyes over mine. Piercing my heart as he fondled both of my ears, his capable hands cradling my cranium, ". . . indeed, sharing a life."

During the month of March 2017, in a private speech to Republican donors at Mar-a-Lago, President Trump said it was great that Chinese President Xi Jinping was able to become "president for life," and that "maybe we'll have to give that a shot someday."

The US Fish and Wildlife service removed the blanket ban originally imposed by the Obama administration on imports of sport-hunted trophies of elephants from certain African countries. The organization also withdrew several Endangered Species Act findings regarding African elephants, lions, and the bontebok antelopes. Roberta Jacobson, the Ambassador to Mexico, resigned from her post.

The White House issued a memorandum stating that transgender personnel were disqualified from military service. The Kremlin announced President Trump's call to congratulate Vladimir Putin on his election victory.

Still saying yes to all things—political events, parties, new relationships with women—was helping me find more Goddesses for my project. People were no longer asking what I did for a living, but rather, "What are you doing about this mess?" This mobilization was consistently activating my personal strength, allowing me to take in bounties of purposeful light. Surely, love was just around the corner.

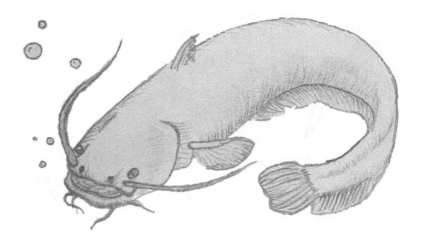

Gone Fishing

Morgan's handle on OkCupid was SoccerMan. He lived in the Sea Cliff area of San Francisco where Robin Williams once resided. He made his living recruiting soccer players internationally. I invited him to a Warriors basketball game with tickets I had secured from a player I'd photographed.

> I'm not a huge fan of basketball or any television sporting events.

Wow, I thought, further evidence that the Scoundrel had not been the greatest choice for me. Mike would shave his full head of hair to sit in the wives' section of the coliseum, and here I was landing these gigs with players and getting comped tickets just six rows from the court. Personally, I could take or leave sporting events, but it was a super impressive date venue.

> I'd much rather sit on your deck with a glass of wine and learn more about you.

Okay, worth a second look.

The following day, when we were to meet, Morgan had been called suddenly to New York to bid on a recruiting job. He sent me a picture of him sitting in an Upper West Side restaurant I recognized, with an over-helping of smoked salmon on his plate, and captioned, "Meeting with Ray of the Manhattan Soccer Club." His face was well-shaped, with high cheekbones topped with a full shock of salt-and-pepper hair. His eyes wore an expression of Viking-like determination and strength. Fifty-five and well over six feet, I would fit nicely in his arms. At this point, just thinking about him and looking at his pictures were enough to keep me responsive.

I was to learn that Morgan was from Estonia, an esoteric Baltic world I knew nothing about, and was raised in Paris. It was his ex-wife, he explained, that had instigated his move to San Francisco so he could be closer to his twenty-three-year-old daughter, whom he adored. Even through texts, I could sense an exotic man I felt I deserved. I am worthy of esoteric, I mused, while filling the bathtub with aromatic gardenia bubbles.

"This might be too good to be true," I thought, as I began to do some Internet investigation. There was indeed a Ray that ran the Manhattan Soccer Club, but Morgan didn't have a Facebook page. Everyone has a Facebook page. From the bathtub, carefully holding my iPhone within safe distance of my nest of foam, I texted him the query.

The next morning, he phoned me, rather than texting. What came across the line was a voice with a glorious French accent.

"You see, my love, I have no use for *theese* Facebook. There *ees* no reason to doubt me. I am real and I eagerly await those fabulous blue eyes of yours."

I froze. As he opened his mouth between sentences, I could hear the gentle smack of tongue against lips. The delicious sensation of his husky, breathy whisper, the uvular trill in the back of his throat set my vulva on fire. I couldn't believe my luck. Naturally, he would have an accent. He was raised in Paris.

Paris, the land of culture and kisses and food. Paris, the city with the balmy romantic outdoor cafés and junk fairs where Alice and I celebrated the deep and familiar adoration of mother and daughter, repairing my brokenness of not having gone with my own mother. Paris, the climax of joyful travel prior to the crest-fall of Rome. Funny how life . . .

"Are you *theere?*"

I inhaled slowly, taking in everything. It was early. The morning fog was silently moving like gossamer silk into my open deck door. I was safe and warm under my botanical quilt. Rick, my pup still on my feet, stood up, circled around three times, and lay back down with a *harumph*.

"Just keep talking," I purred. "Don't stop talking." I slid my hand between my warm legs. I had gone straight from bath to bed the prior evening and my body was still fragrant and soggy clean.

Masturbating is not a common practice for me. I like the real thing, but I was untethered and yearning. Wetting my middle two fingers on my tongue I spread open my labia so one finger rested on either side of my clitoris and squeezed gently.

Morgan chuckled; I squeezed harder.

"Well, I have good news."

I started moving my hand in a clockwise circle.

"I have landed the contract and I will be making a lot of *moneys*. I'm very excited."

"Me too." I quickened my assist, pushing harder on my chakra, my back naturally arching. "Hold on. I'm gonna put you on speaker phone," I whispered. I needed two hands.

I set my phone on the pillow beside me, ensuring the volume was maximized and returned to the task at hand.

"Go on." I breathed.

You deserve this, I chanted silently. I brought my other hand down to force my legs to open wider. I could smell my own earthy nectar, a distillation of urgency, abandon, and self-love. I was soaking the sheets with my happy vulva. My hips now were gyrating, throbbing, and grinding into my own hands, I imagined I was in a barrel on the top of the falls. The top, the top. Oh God . . . Oh God . . . I felt three sudden jerks as I released with pleasure. My breath ushered the barrel down the thrilling falls slow-motion, filling my senses with oxygen all the way to my fingertips. Rick let out a deep sigh.

"Doxology" was the first word to enter my brain. Funny how . . .

"Are you still *theere*? What's going on. Did you hear me?"

It was too soon in the relationship to tell this voice on the phone what had just happened.

"You got the contract! *Hoorah!* Let's celebrate! Will you be home to-night?"

"They're sending me to Beijing. I leave in the morning."

"What? You have to come back to San Francisco first and get your things." This was not fair.

"I will have my things sent. It will only take eight weeks. Tell me you will wait for me. This contract is valuable. We'll have all the time in the world when I get home."

I pictured us on the beach outside his house that cantilevered over crashing waves. One of my famous picnics sprawled before us. His head in my lap singing French love songs to me as I fed him figs.

"I'll wait."

For reasons beyond the rational, the more time I spent concentrating on Morgan, the more lost in him I became. For the following eight weeks, I lived for the sound of the Viber ring. Viber is yet another way to text, and the preferred application for those dialoguing internationally. It's a purple "V" on my phone that when transmitting an incoming call makes a low, dull *bong, bong* sound like the bell frogs of southern Costa Rica.

Morgan would reach out only after 4:00 p.m., and until 6:00 a.m., according to the time difference, and when the bell frog rang, I would lunge across the table to hear that French accent tell me everything I wanted to hear: "It's just a feeling I have, baby. I want to love you like no other and take care of you for the rest of your life. When I get home, I won't need to work for another six months and we can do whatever you want." Another photo would ensue, this time him wearing his heavy pea coat in the cold Beijing morning. "Promise me you will take your profile down and wait for me. I need to harvest fifteen players, and I've got six already. It won't be long."

I would stand at the kitchen window slowly drying a plate and gaze into the distance, my eyes drifting down toward Warren's surmounting garden, now with untold numbers of beehives, wondering what my wardrobe decision would be for picking him up from the airport. I couldn't walk in heels, but I could carry a pair to the gate. There, I would stop short, as our eyes met, then, setting down his suitcase, his eyes never leaving mine, we would run, slow-motion, into a cinematic embrace.

"Those weights are too heavy for you," my Pilates instructor at the club admonished.

"I want to be in tip-top shape for my new beau when he returns from Beijing."

I'd now spent over a hundred dollars on several cagey negligees from the British Boudoir Boutique. I was telling all my friends about Morgan and how lucky I was to find him.

"This is absurd," Scoundrel snorted, one morning in the studio. "You haven't even met the guy and you're making plans. He's probably going to end up being short."

Through everything, Mike continued to be adorable. He had broken my heart, displaced me and all of my belongings, betrayed me openly, yet was acting like some kind of cheerleader for me. He was still paying my health insurance, my car lease, and the rent for the studio, and the country club still considered us a couple.

"You're doing too much for this guy. Has he sent you flowers, yet?"

We ran into each other at the studio at least twice a week. When I had a client, I would text Mike, and he would give leniency for that and cede some of his office time. Otherwise, we were frequently working in tandem in our shared studio space. He would tell me news of his dog, his girlfriend, and the next big concert or travel plans. I would tell him stories about my dating, about the happenings at the Drama Farm. We had friends in common and that needed to be discussed. He would admonish me if he thought someone wasn't good enough for me and I would do the same regarding the Mortgage Broker.

"Mike? Why isn't she taking care of you? That looks like a pretty bad injury." Mike was often injured due to his reckless lifestyle: skateboarding through traffic, skiing double-black diamond slopes, chopping wood, cleaning rooftops, driving drunk and fast. My love for him had always been like that between a mother and son, sex being a borderline-incestuous side dish. The sex now was long gone, obviously the right choice, though holding his hand and caring for his well-being was hard to let go of. I supposed he held some leftover feelings as well, thus the gentle letdown.

My twenty-six-year-old son, Henry, and I were working together at the time on the marketing for the Goddess Project. We sat in his Walnut Creek apartment working on the website, logo, and mission statement. I would tell him of Morgan and his adventures in Beijing.

"Mom, you're coming on pretty strong, you know. You haven't even met him yet."

But, as we listened to music while working, I came across a folk-pop duo, "The Well Pennies," who narrated my dizzy, happy feelings, so I started sending YouTube recordings to Morgan. He loved them. I sent him images of me riding horses on the beach in Pacifica, getting ready for the Oakland Indie Awards, and long walks in the woods with Rick, my dog.

Things were changing at Warren's Drama Farm. I was attending every powerful women's gathering and meeting leaders and changemakers, making connections with powerhouses of Planned Parenthood, pollution-blockers, and congresswomen, while Warren was fervently planting his garden from seed, using the kitchen and living room as his nursery. I found this compulsion endearing, yet every surface of the house was covered with soil, spilling six cells of sprouts in various stages, making it difficult to maneuver around to work or, God forbid, share a meal. The surplus of supplies of his handiwork—bunches of cedar siding, stray lumber, an old, used pond, an occasional ship's wheel or bed set—littered the driveway and house to the point that it became impossible to plug in my electric car. He would clean it up, then like a tornado, the materials would be strewn again in a day. The chicken coop he talked of building sat by the door in its packaging for months. The table saw infringed on our living space next to the plethora of bongos, and his food shopping never slowed. I counted thirty-seven cans of lima beans, yet he kept coming home with more. I still admired this creative man, but he began to turn, changing his mind about allowing me to be involved with his daughter, and withdrawing. Some days he would stay in bed all day.

Molly, as well, was losing her footing. At one point, a friend of hers called me while I was at a political rally and insisted I race home. When I did, I found Molly in a heap on her bed, incapacitated with anxiety. I was to stay with her until her mother, Mandy, came in from Reno to calm her.

"Tell me what's happening, darling? I want to help." I spoke in the most soothing tone I could muster, setting my "Not My President" sign down. I was still wearing my hand-knit pussy hat.

Molly's eyes darted around as if she was desperately trying to remember where she had put something inordinately important. Her hands had become icy, closed blossoms from hyperventilating.

"I don't, I can't, I can't decide." Crawling into bed with her, I rocked her in my arms until her mother showed up. Mandy looked as if she had run the whole distance from Reno to Oakland in sandals.

After Molly was soothed to sleep, Mandy and I sat in the living room to talk.

"She didn't want you and Warren to know. She was doing so well."

Apparently this dissent was new to me, but not to Molly or her mother.

When things got bad, Warren would do some outlandishly dynamic thing, like bring in a swarm of bees and build another hive, or roast coffee in a new kitchen gadget. At one point we had over ten working hives. No honey was ever harvested; I just found a lot of misguided honeybees buzzing in my bed on hot evenings. Our once fluid and nurturing environment was feeling manic and dysfunctional. We tried joining a drumming circle, which seemed to bring us all together, but that, too, went by the wayside. Mandy was apparently going to stay until Molly—unable to function without her—could feel stabilized, so she slept in the same bed with her daughter.

Mandy liked to clean, demanding balance where there was none. I would come home to find her knee-deep in cans of butter beans and artichoke hearts, moldy potatoes and beets, attacking the corners of the pantry with a toothbrush.

"Rick died," I bled to Morgan over Viber. He didn't answer, as it was nighttime in Beijing. Losing my pup, a gift from Neil Young's sound man, was profound. For the past sixteen years, my handsome silky shepherd had been at my flank with undying faithfulness. He accompanied me everywhere—in the car, on the trail, at the studio, on locations. I was never alone with Rick, his chin on my knee, or shoulder, or foot, depending on how I was postured. When licking my children's bare legs, he would hold his tongue still on their salty skin mid-stroke for as long as he could to take in the blissful flavor of his pack. Everyone loved Rick. I was so proud of his remarkable beauty, inside and out. To the very end, he was my bright red meridian.

On his last day, after a four-mile historical walking tour, Rick was bushed. I lifted his sixty-five pounds to my bed where he slept all night, then took him out early to pee. Old dogs pee a lot, often zig-zagging a path as they walk; they also drink like camels, which he did right before he rested, letting the pure light take him from me. It was just like him not to trouble anyone. The sky was a dazzling promise of orangey-pink. The stillness, deafening and profound.

I texted Dani, since we'd previously made a date to go to church, as an experiment.

> I still want to do church, but Rick has died.

> Oh baby. I'll be right there.

I woke the house up to pow-wow on the best process and settled on cremation. Dani and I in church clothes, Warren in a soccer shirt and wrinkled boxers, Molly in an incomplete fur jacket she'd been stitching, the hem dangling like a furry tail, and her mother, Mandy, in the oldest flannel nightgown I'd ever seen, unbuttoned in the back, with a Victorian semicircle of faded roses and lace around her neck rallied. Each taking a corner, we carried Rick's lifeless body to the car in a Mexican blanket.

Dani and I dropped his body off at the vet's, then numbly sat through a blurry church service that offered up nothing. I stopped at a street vendor booth on Telegraph and bought a bright red gemstone to keep in my pocket. So final, so solid, so sad, yet, so right.

The Drama Farm was empty when I returned, which was just what I wanted. On my bed was a perfect watercolor likeness of my Rick on acid-free cottony-soft paper, with the caption, "Sweet Ricky." Molly's genius at work, again. I made an altar with the image, Rick's bone-shaped dog tag, his polka-dotted collar, and the red bandana that always looked so striking draped around his strong, tricolored chest. Holding the kerchief to my face, I inhaled my old pup one last time. The end of that sweet, musky era of loving an old animal. The end of a gigantic parcel of my life with the nicest guy ever.

"Thank you," I whispered.

Just then, my Pandora station offered up the slower, remastered version of Joni singing *Both Sides Now*, the one she'd recorded with the symphony when she was significantly older and wiser than she was when she had originally strummed it. Honestly, there is nothing older and wiser than Joni Mitchell at any age. Her work is the gospel soundtrack of my life.

I lay my head on the kitchen counter in relief and wept violently for a full five minutes, my tears exposing and relieving my beleaguered heart.

Indeed, something is lost and something is gained in living every day, Joni reminded, opening me to the cavernous mystery. I envisioned my Ricky-Roo on the beach in untethered joy, a sand-encrusted tennis ball resting on his way-too-long tongue.

Sixteen years is beyond grace.

I rode the feeling, leaning deeply into the painful void, and allowed the ribbony music to escort me to restful gratitude.

When I lifted my head, snot webbing between me and the beige countertop, I turned to find Sashy looking at me as if I were naked. She'd been at her mother's that morning and had missed this chapter at the Drama Farm, but I guessed that Warren had told her.

"What do we do?" her prepubescent expression asked. There is so much for a young girl to learn from other women in her tribe. She had turned to me countless times for navigational tools that her father didn't have in his big leathery belt.

"I'm alright," I assured her.

Taking her in my arms, the crown of her head fit sublimely under my chin, and she turned her head as if to listen to my heart like a conch that might give her an ocean to guide her. The embrace was long and comforting. We rocked, inhaling each other's capacity for reciprocal relief. Warm light filled in the cracks like molten gold.

On week eight of our relationship, Morgan called me, I thought to give me his flight itinerary, but instead to let me know there was a glitch. The Chinese government had levied him a huge tax on transporting the fifteen players he'd finally found, and he couldn't cover the bill.

"Are you asking me for money?"

"Yes, I need four thousand dollars."

I hung up the phone.

For the first time ever, I opted to smoke in bed. I texted Warren, Molly, and Mandy in tandem and let them know that my secret soccer agent had been exposed as a scam.

I'm so sorry.

> We love you.

While I was writhing in bed, squandering my workday to sorrow, Tony texted.

> Hey what's going on with the Goddess Project? Come down and tell me a story.

> I can't. I have experienced an emotional fall and plan to stay in bed all day.

> No, come down!! Sounds like you've got another story for me.

Pulling on a pair of sweats, a running bra, and a hand-me-up flannel shirt from my daughter, I drove down the hill to the village. Halfway down the block, Scoundrel's garage door was open to display the pool table, surrounded by several guy friends. I heard the crack of a solid break, followed by a happy roar. I could make out the AC/DC song pounding the bucolic neighborhood with imposing lyrics, and knocking everyone out with those American thighs!

I slowed. Mike would care that Rick died. He should know, and we should hug about it, but this was not the time. I rolled down the window to wave to Mike's lifelong cronies that I'd learned to tolerate, if not love.

"Hey Reenster! *Whaz-up?* Come play with us!" Don shouted.

This cast of characters knew Scoundrel for what he was and all admired him for his feral lifestyle. They'd been playing together since they were children—carousing the neighborhood, stealing street signs to display in the garage, delighting in games and beer at inappropriate hours. They knew he'd jilted me, but looked at me as if to say, "Hey, you wouldn't want him any other way, would you?"

I smiled, remembering how I'd worried about the neighbor's concern about "The Loud House," and wondered again how Mike always landed on his feet.

"We'll get together later," I lied. "I've got an appointment right now."

I was so happy to see solid Tony, who greeted me with a long hug I was able to cry into.

"Jesus, what's up? I heard about Ricky. Gosh, I'm sorry, but he was so old, Reenie."

While I was touched so lovingly by my platonic friend, I told him of losing a dog and a false front romance in the same week. How I'd been scammed, how stupid I had been and how ashamed I was.

Morgan, my son Henry had explained, is what is called a "catfisher." Henry showed me that there was an entire television show on this topic. Naturally, there was. This was why I didn't watch television.

"You're not ready to come down from this," Tony consoled me. "Try this on. What if we scammed the scammer? Tell him you can get him the money and string him along until you feel strong enough to let him go."

This seemed like a good idea. With a paralyzed heart, I texted Morgan letting him know that I'd get him the money. First, though, I'd need to see his passport, which he effortlessly produced with the obvious assistance of Photoshop. I'm a photographer. I can see a photographic alteration from twenty feet. My heart was broken. Beyond the letdown of my crest-fallen future, I realized that my need for love was so great that I had allowed myself to be fooled by something so obviously false. I had put aside common sense for a pipe dream. I had pleasured myself to ecstasy for a fake. How embarrassing.

> Now! A picture of yourself right now, please, with a paper star cut out and held up to your forehead.

This he obviously could not manage. For another week, we continued to dialogue about our lovers' plans, once we got through this mess and he was able to return safely to San Francisco, where he lived next door to where Robin Williams had lived. His urgency to get his money was mounting.

> My daughter needs me
> for her wedding.

I was acutely aware that a wedding would cost him well over four thousand dollars, as would a hotel room in Beijing. The math did not add up. The lies smarted more deeply each day, building a stealthy callous on my heart. When, at last, I was able to accept the fact that I had been a fool, and that, in reviewing the last eight weeks of my mist, was able to discern why my heart would even lean this way, I sent what was to be my *Dear John* text.

> Morgan, I know you are
> a catfisher. I'm not going
> to send you any money.
> Yet I need to ask you.
> Why did you take so long
> to ask for money? I really
> fell in love with you, and
> honestly, I think you
> loved me too. This line of
> work must be painful. Is
> it worth it?

Rather than texting, for the first time in this long idiosyncratic course, he video-called me. What I saw on my phone, lying there in my big, king-sized bed on the top of the Oakland hills, bees buzzing around my lit-up phone, was not Morgan. Not the tall, chiseled French man born in Estonia and soon returning to his house in San Francisco's tony Sea Cliff to lift me up and save me. What I saw was a very young, very beautiful African man, seemingly about thirty years old, with compassionate brown saucer eyes. Behind him, I could see a dingy plaster wall covered in cracks and loose electrical cable, apparently taped or nailed to the wall in classic Dr. Seuss fashion.

"Of course, I love you." The heavy French accent completely perplexed me now. "You are beautiful. You have a wonderful life. You go to glamorous events, you live in the mountains, you ride horses on the ocean. I am black. I have nothing. I am in Nigeria."

Whah!? My mind flashed to the news revealing the Boko Haram kidnapping Nigerian schoolgirls, the sexual mutilation and death. Villages of uncounted, underserved people.

Wow.

The shock was terrific, as my brain threw me a thousand neuronic problems to solve at once.

Okay.

This aspect of a man was created by another man. By pretending to be the kind of man that I might want, he could make money.

Morgan?

Yes, Morgan. You've been scammed.

But I love Morgan.

But he's not real.

The man I know is real.

He lied.

Wow. But I don't have any money. I was kind of hoping he did.

Kachink.

Wait. Wait. Wait. By looking at myself through the eyes of this child, I was not, as I had thought, unable to take care of myself. I was not frail and without direction, in need of this figment, Morgan, to give me a platform.

Notice who you are, girl, and rejoice in the abundance that lives there. Never again surrender to scarcity. The words came like a solved riddle.

Through his eyes, I could see my life differently. I was in contrast, wealthy, with boundless resources at my fingertips. Sure, I'd been dumped, yet I was a confident woman, living in one of the finest corners of the world. My work, my attachments, and relationships were valuable beyond words. I had created this benevolent life, as precarious as it was, and damned if I was going to squander it. Relativity and compassion filled me with the need to explore.

In the weeks that followed, more was revealed about my cyber lover. His name was not Morgan, but Sunday, like Robinson Crusoe's Man Friday. He was most likely named this as it was the day of the week he was born.

I opted to continue our relationship on the phone, no longer with the intention of finding a lover who was going to rescue me, but, rather, a friend who explained for me a life in a place I would more than likely never know. It was important to me that he understood this romance wasn't going to happen—not only was eight thousand miles a hefty commute, but our lives were different. It was most definitely not because he was black. Poverty is not fair, and the fact that he was stuck there should have nothing to do with his skin. "It's your government." We spent hours talking in the night about politics. I explained our system, while he explained his.

"Yours is a better idea, this House and Senate system."

"Evening-out the powers that be is the idea," I tried, "but power, in nature, doesn't wish to be controlled. The man in charge of our country right now is a real problem. I often feel like we are on a child's playground. He is a bully."

I set him up with an online coding class, got the address of his village, and sent him an extra-large T-shirt with a bear hugging the state of California. We talked of cheese and I attempted a delivery of Dutch Gouda to him, which was no doubt lifted along the way. I felt hopeful that he would push through his coding assignments and better himself.

One day, I mused, I might meet him in New York and recognize him on the street—a self-made man, wearing a button-up, striped shirt. We would sit in a cafe and discuss world politics.

But it was not to be. Eventually, communication drifted away into the ether. It's just too painful, we both agreed.

"We will keep our Viber handle and stay in touch," I assured him.

"And I will wait for your Goddess Book. Maybe one day you will write about me."

"Yes, Sunday."

Drying off in the locker room at the club, I told my story to a fellow yoga partner.

"Oh, my mother has one of those," she consoled. "She actually sends him money so she can have someone to talk to. It's really sick how lonely someone can be, isn't it?"

I opened the door to the sauna, laid my towel on the hot wood, and stretched out my long torso onto the fragrant cedar. Inhaling the warmth, I thought of my mother, and asked her spirit to join me.

When I ask, she always enters. She'd never left us, not for a moment. Sometimes I drive up the windy road to the vista where she and Dad are buried and lay on top of their side-by-side graves for hours and talk. Sometimes I cry, sometimes I laugh, but I always feel engulfed in immense love and assuredness. I don't need to be there, though, I can be anywhere to recapture the *womby* sensation that uplifts me. Mom would laugh at me now over this last fiasco. Lying there in the hot sauna, I laughed for her and with her. Reeling in her memory, I could hear her voice echoing in the hallways of my heart.

To understand love, we need to understand the chemistry of the brain. Although it's just a matter of hormones responding to certain actions, sensing that someone gives a shit about you can change your whole day. Someone disappearing can likewise mess with you in a way that haunts your every movement. "Ghosting," it is called—a change of heart, perhaps interest somewhere else. For some reason, it is just not a relationship meant to be. Love can be buoyant, or it can be devastating. Just the sound of a text coming in and a name of someone you fancy flashing up creates and enlivens a gleam. A neuron triggers a splash of dopamine.

Texting is a brain hack. Serotonin, which the brain produces in situations of sunlight, exercise, laughter, and functional relationships, produces contentment and happiness, whereas dopamine is delivered from pleasure—sugar, cigarettes, and texting. Dopamine highs become increasingly hard to maintain, requiring more frequent hits, until neurons finally, in unsatisfied frustration, burn out. Staying in tune and clear on every feeling coming down the stream is essential in learning how it is that you really want to feel. I opted to leave my phone alone and get more exercise. I took up birdwatching.

Put a Bird on It

On our second photo session of Goddesses, Emily came armed with more wonderful treasures. For this group, I had assembled a shaman, some Native American women, the Executive Director of Artists United, a Cantor, a healer, a two-time breast cancer survivor, a Baptist singer, a spearheading educator, the Mayor of Oakland Libby Schaaf, and my very own crusader on the fight against homelessness—my daughter, Alice. I had been talking about the project at a party a few weeks earlier, and wondered out loud where I might obtain a taxidermy owl. As providence continued flowing through me, a woman overhearing the conversation remarked, "I have one. I work with the forestry department."

The studio was a flurry of flowing dresses, giant headdresses, and intense feminine energy. Emily was styling and powdering like a zephyr, somersaulting from one end of the room to the other. Each woman had some kind of object that was to demonstrate her power. The women brought flowers from a garden, a bow and arrow, the Torah, a Prussian sword; one brought her mother's handcrafted ceramic bowl. Then one gal extracted a tiny plastic cat out of her bag. The room stopped chatting and exploded with laughter.

"What the hell is that? Power from a plastic cat?"

"I guess I didn't understand," she whimpered.

I scanned the table full of items Emily had brought and my eyes rested on a very large ornate candleholder with a lovely, scrolled handle. Our eyes met, and she grabbed a large, bird-shaped candle.

"Here," she announced, setting it on the large, round platform, "put a bird on that!"

From that day forward, this was to be our creative solution to all things dysfunctional. As life continued to give us Donald Trump, scammers, and liars, as we perpetually waded through this muck of preposterous decisions and blindness to truth and justice—to this, we put a bird on it.

The bird says, "Look, chin up, we've got this because we collectively look with love, and fucking LOVE, God Damn It, will win!"

After four hours of exhausting yet exhilarating work, I crashed into the nearest chair and surveyed the mess. My studio was ravaged from our sacred dress-up party. Native feathers, drums, and gemstones, Gothic leather sword scabbards, and wrist cuffs festooned every available surface. I took in the unique satisfaction one only gets from being with women, and, with a silent chuckle, began to clean up. The plastic cat had been left, and with a pang, I hoped we hadn't hurt the feelings of the First Female Physiology Teacher in Oakland.

Scoundrel would be returning to the studio the following morning and would no doubt make fun of my project. This project felt so close to my heart. I just didn't have room for his cynicism to squash my passion and magic. As tired as I was, it was important that I sequester as much costumery as possible. Hanging the layers of silky dresses in the studio closet, I noticed the waxy bird that Emily had carefully placed on a tall stack of printed material. I had worn through an entire ink cartridge printing what looked like an opus of a manuscript, one well over seventy pages and practically two-inches thick. A heavy, tidy stack of texting dialogue from Viber. I had marveled at the heft of the pile and enjoyed how comprehensively it told a story that I didn't want to forget: my dialogue with Morgan, or Sunday, or whatever I was to remember him as. I thought I had hidden this heap on a shelf in the closet, yet Em had been following my affair and knew well my fallen crest. My friend, my stylist, my wing woman had somehow found it, and with her quiet, intuitive wink, reminded me to put a bird on it.

In April of 2017, President Trump delivered a speech to North America's Building Trades Unions announcing the removal of construction regulations on the building of the Keystone XL Pipeline. Following a chemical attack in Syria which killed numerous civilians, Trump blamed the Obama administration for not doing more to regulate chemical weapons, yet he delivered an address to the National Rifle Association reiterating his guarantee of Second Amendment rights. The Department of State cut funding to the UN Population Fund, a fund focused on reproductive health and family planning, while Trump signed a bill into law nullifying a regulation that disallowed states to withhold money from abortion providers. A Tax March took place to protest the President's refusal to turn over his taxes, to which he tweeted, "The election is over." All this, as his self-imposed deadline for production of a White House report into Russian interference in the 2016 election expired.

As spring gently waltzed into my fugitive heart, I was soothed by the changing colors of the Oakland Hills. The familiar curves turned minty green with daffodils erupting from every available roadside and median. Deer fawned in plain sight and *Time* magazine's cover asked, "Is Truth Dead?" Good question, and the one paramount to me at this turn of personal growth. I'd been scammed. This pierced what I'd always felt was a bubble of safety. Yet this previous safety was itself something of an untruth. At any moment, someone I leaned upon could vanish, and vanish they did. Who was I to rely on? Where was I to land? I spent much time pondering my own strength: this new knowledge that my life was interesting and glamorous to an outsider. My desire to stay present intensified in the faith that my truth would emerge in love.

Picnic

Many of my fond memories are wrapped around the picnic. Any opportunity to gather feels salubrious when done outside. Grandma and Grandpa could assemble a picnic in no time, as can I. A picnic is a decorative blanket, usually a 1940s embroidered gem in a wicker basket with a lid. Opening the lid reveals treasures of exotic cheeses and berries, bread and salami or roast chicken, always an apple, and, on lucky occasions, oysters. Since I took over the ritual, wine, pate, an artichoke, and cornichons or olives have become essential. Planning the feast is nearly as fun as the actual spreading out of the alfresco before my captive audience. Nothing kills joy more than food on paper or plastic. So, although the basket tends to be heavy, I always use the good dishes and silver.

One of my favorite picnic locations is on the banks of our downtown lake, named after an historic figure, Samuel Merritt. In the 1870s, he owned a substantial plot of land in what is now downtown Oakland, and wanting his mansion to have a lake, he dammed a part of the estuary and created one three miles in diameter. His mansion, this still-standing architectural wonder, conspicuously towers over Lake Merritt, and, being an history enthusiast, I love to explore the happenings during the turn of the century. Merritt's mansion is named the Camron-Stanford House for the few families that bought it from him. This Victorian edifice and I have a relationship, and on some Sundays, I give historical tours through what is now a landmark. I have a free parking spot, which makes transporting even the heaviest basket a breeze.

A perfect, grassy knoll astride the dancing water, and happy poetic ghosts of Bret Harte, Mark Twain, John Muir, and Jack London color the day. When I am sprawled there, I feel as if I am a player in a Seurat painting. Stretching out long upon the grass, I think, this is a perfect date location. A nice place to explore the curiosities of men.

Rory was British and absolutely hilarious. He had classic childhood stories of sneaking up on Uncle Ned and frolicking in the English garden of hollyhocks and delphiniums. I envisioned him, a small boy with knickers on, conferring with a hedgehog and bunny rabbit. Rory lived too far south, and we met once in Pacifica for a meal, then for a few of these picnics. Though I urged him several times to meet me again, as I loved his stories and fancied him a great ornament at dinner parties, he, like so many others, ghosted away. I'm not sure what it would have been like to have had more of a relationship with him. We so enjoyed conversing and he made me laugh, but he obviously didn't have the hunger for a partner that I did. No . . . "there, there," was the general feeling. When trying to imagine kissing him, which never happened, I didn't feel the butterflies, the desire necessary. He lacked physicality. He did have two children, somehow. Perhaps they were delivered by the proverbial stork.

Orion lived in a rather tony house in San Anselmo, across a bridge about an hour north. A Southeast Asian raised in Germany, his accent was rhythmic and chalky. He was shocked by the United States' political climate, and therefore, was working diligently on an online truth-in-reporting salon. He urged me to add content to his feed and help him get funds to bring his platform to the next stage, advertising.

After a picnic, we walked around Lake Merritt and discussed how my potential philanthropic contacts might help. I drove the distance to his house twice. Full of exotic and expensive art, his sprawling rancher felt staged. His elusive daughters shared a room so tidy and pristine, with un-loved stuffed animals lined up like little soldiers, that I wondered if the girls were pure figment. "Perhaps I could meet them one day," I considered. Orion worked tirelessly on his Salon Project, up all night finding and posting honest news. "I just need some investors so I can hire more staff," he said. It felt like such an important idea as we were all scrambling to do whatever we could to bring order to our political disarray. I didn't feel love for this man, but his project felt right, and I'd been so embarrassed about our country's blind decisions that his vision gave me something positive to work toward. I called upon my prominent friends to meet with him.

"How do you know this man?" Erwin spoke gently to me at the tea shop. I had scheduled a meeting with Orion and my brilliant friend. Erwin was nearing ninety years old, and frequently had an oxygen tank on wheels nearby. Like Ruth Bader Ginsburg, his remaining time on our planet was carefully guarded by all who knew him, his wisdom was a guiding star. He had invented the algorithm or some such thing in the '50s. A wing at Cal Berkeley and a foundation was named for him and his wife, Sally. I had photographed his lovely extended family on a few occasions and found them all to be old-world, solid, and smart. I called on Erwin when there were ACLU and other important fundraisers, as he cared deeply for jus-tice. After a thirty-minute elevator speech, Orion excused himself awkwardly. It was clear that his idea was not well-received by my gracious friend.

I explained to Erwin that I'd met Orion on OkCupid, a site he'd never heard of. Erwin's eyes softened as I spoke, like those of a great mystical whale. The blue cataracts could not conceal his loving circumspection and protection. I wouldn't say Erwin and I were close friends, yet having lost my parents so early, I felt very drawn to his acumen and treasured all the wisdom and advice that fell from his lips.

"The paradigm is changing, Reenie. You'll need to be more vigilant with the company you keep. Check the facts on everyone."

Eventually, Orion asked me to invest twenty thousand dollars. I shied away. Indeed, within a few weeks, we were estranged, and when I looked up his site, the work was gone. Erwin had been correct. I wondered what it felt like to be Orion and what his parents were like. Had they been renegades and liars?

Randy wanted to be called Randall, but he clearly wasn't a Randall, so I settled on "Rand." A handsome, scruffy, New Age Man who dropped in, hung out, and got real, Rand was settled in a sweet South Oakland house and took pride in his involvement in a radical men's group that chanted and drummed together.

He was still in disbelief that his last girlfriend had dropped out. "Her loss," he pouted.

I wore my big red, twenty-four-inch sun hat and a dress when we went to Ocean Beach for the day. I brought my trademark picnic with oysters and cheese. It was one of those remarkably clear and warm days on the edge of California's continent. We talked about his men's group and I told him my European story and my journey in search of a new confidence in the universe. Afterward, we drove to a coffee shop for a poetry slam, where I stood and read some Ina Coolbrith and Rand read some Rumi (not the same piece read to me over a massage, but still good). It was all quite dreamy.

The following evening, Rand informed me of a party going on not far from me.

> I'm busy until ten, but I'll swing by.

The house was a gigantic mid-century piece consisting of what felt like at least four stories perched high upon the hill. I had been shooting a wedding and was dying for a glass of wine, so I headed straight for the kitchen. There was a table laden high with half-eaten sliders, empty hummus containers, and several water bottles. No booze. This was puzzling, because everyone looked pretty loose, actually, *beyond* loose, they looked downright high.

Circles of five-to-ten people were in locked formations like the loveball orgies one witnesses at newt ponds in January. Some were dancing, others just kind of gyrating. When I finally found Rand, he was sharing some kind of magic beam or supersonic secret with another fellow, their eyes locked.

I concluded acid or MDMA, and when I parted some inviting velvet curtains into the den, all this and more was going on . . . sans clothing. Gender or age did not appear to be a factor here. These people seemed to play very well in groups. As each partygoer took turns being the star of the cuddle-puddle, there were long embraces and stroking where I couldn't tell whose arms and legs were whose. I took a step closer, trying to appear inconspicuous and mask my expression of complete incredulousness. No one seemed to notice me, and for a moment I wished I could be invisible. Hard to do fully clothed, with my jacket still in my arms.

Just then, a naked, smallish man walked toward me, his pendulous ball sack swinging side to side, and extended his hand toward me. I wanted to be polite, and heck, I was here. I might as well be present, right?

"You are untethered," I tried to convince myself. "Perhaps there is something in you that can be explored." Yet, try as I might, I couldn't make myself find this activity sexually stirring, at all.

Mister Ball Sack looked deeply into my eyes and whispered, "you are safe here."

"Poor guy," I thought. That's all I could think—poor guy. I'd wager that he had an ex-wife somewhere, perhaps here.

In slow motion, he danced his arms around my shoulders and moved in for a kiss, which I clumsily accepted, then, with the most loving smile I could render, pulled away and retreated from the den.

"What the hell is everyone on?" I said, as I interrupted Rand's affair.

I didn't know Rand that well, yet he was the only one there I knew to ask.

"It's honesty and pure love," he cooed.

He seemed ridiculous to me, as did this whole wobbly crew. Not that I was against honesty and love, I simply felt a few steps had been overlooked, like perhaps, dinner and a movie.

"Who do I gotta fuck to get a drink around here?" I joked, trying to be light-humored and nonplussed by what was clearly an orgy.

My humor was lost on Rand, who gave me an airy expression of "perhaps one day you'll understand, but you are obviously constrained by your personal baggage."

I went to my car, and fishing in the dark behind the passenger seat, found the bottle of champagne I had been gifted from the wedding. I'd hoped to save it and enjoy it with Molly back at the Drama Farm, but this was just too bizarre to miss. I went back into the large house and settled on the top of the stairs as voyeur, setting the heavy bottle on my knee between fizzy swigs. I took off my shoes and socks and rubbed my feet. It had been a long day, photographing through tears of joy, a young couple proclaiming their everlasting promise to stand together, forever. I'd captured the expressions of hopeful assuredness and solid commitment to family and tribe.

In contrast, what I was absorbing before me at this love fest was not love at all, but rather a competition of who honestly could care less than the next. A complete risk of the human heart, not to mention venereal disease. Judging was not my job and watching this carnal dance didn't disturb me at all, because watching it gave me a bit of light into my boundaries and desires.

A few days later, I brought some artichokes over to Rand's house and he gave me a coconut massage, but he never kissed me. Within a week, he had ghosted. I suppose I was too square for him, or maybe he'd been ensnared by a newt-woman (or man) at one of his emotionless parties.

Men like Rand are all around us. Often the product of hippy parents and men's groups, they work hard to be gentle people. Workshops and retreats guide them through what I sense might be inner pain or an unfilled chasm. These men are soft, they dance and call other men "brother." Not wishing to hurt anyone or anything, they are often in tune with the feminine, theirs and that of the women in their lives. Like all men, they are complicated and fragile. I felt I accidentally hurt Rand's feelings by not experimenting with polyamory, yet honestly, we just weren't attracted to each other. How could you have an open relationship if you didn't even have a relationship at all? I ran into him one more time at the Hardly Strictly Bluegrass festival later that summer when I was on another date. We awkwardly murmured hello as he faded behind the Gordon Biersch brew stand.

The Tiger Tamer

I nicknamed Bill "The Tiger Tamer," because, quite literally, he was a retired animal handler. Working for Africa USA, he was in charge of two Siberian Tigers, which he wrestled with to the delight of big crowds.

"Well, I guess he's come out of retirement," my friends teased, referring to my recently acclaimed vociferous appetite for dating.

Our first tryst was on the marina in Jack London Square in Oakland, where he explained over beer and artichoke pizza that his OkCupid handle was "ShouldBWriting," because he was in the throes of writing a memoir about his experiences with these animals.

He was nicely put together, with dazzling blue eyes and one of those kisses that makes you wonder; we decided to pursue our acquaintance.

He'd made the decision that our next meeting would be at a Peruvian restaurant on College Avenue in Berkeley. I was racing in from an artist's gathering of filmmakers in Fremont, ten miles away, and feeling high in my short red romper and cowboy boots. My automated Australian male

Siri voice narrated navigation through my car. "In three hundred feet, turn left on 40th Street." I asked my car to text Bill that I was five minutes away, as I turned left on what I felt certain was a green light.

The next few minutes were a blur. Looking up, I saw the face of a young African American woman in an oncoming early model Honda. As she slammed on her breaks, her face expressed, "What the fuck?!" Without enough time to avoid the impact, she crashed into the right rear side of my car. We pulled over to exchange insurance, contact info, and a long hug, expressing gratitude that we were still alive. I texted Bill to let him know there was yet another delay and rallied my injured vehicle into the parking lot.

When I arrived at the restaurant, I was rattled from the accident and it took me some time to calm down. Bill stood up from the table and gave me a long embrace, then setting his forehead on mine, gazed deeply into my eyes, blue on blue. His kiss was like an affirmation, and I strained to hold onto it.

Bill was a gentleman. Well-bred and well-read. We could converse for hours over a meal, leading into the late night, where he would then lead me with his velvety paws, claws retracted, to his bed.

It was providential that Bill had worked with tigers, as he was essentially a big cat. Sitting on his solitary bluff, he would quietly survey his kingdom, his eyes panning the savannah of his life and thinking about the wife, the falcon handler whom he had recently cremated after more than a decade of her languishing battle with cancer.

I'd hoped that I might be the next giraffe he'd have dominion over, though I often wondered if he was hungry at all. He rarely returned texts. Yet, when engaged with the pride, he was all-in. Crawling toward me on all fours, a shock of blonde hair falling over his forehead, his gaze was mesmerizing.

We saw each other for weeks and took up Tuesday salsa at a downtown club. Naturally, he was a lovely dancer.

"I know someone you know," he said one morning, as he caressed my hip in his bedroom after bringing me a perfect frothy latte.

He owned a house twenty minutes east of the Drama Farm that had been neglected from the grief of his sick wife. Now that she had died, he spoke of throwing away the musty, poorly framed art, filling in the broken swimming pool, and creating a yard. The plan was that I would help. Helping men fix up their places was becoming a pattern.

"The gal I told you I was going to cool off on when I met you. Apparently, she is a client of yours."

When he named her, I blew coffee out of my nose. Cindy Brown? Beautiful, graceful, ageless Cindy Brown? I recalled photographing her and her lovely, then-teenaged girl, a dancer. Cindy lived in a charming Maybeck house in Berkeley. As far as I was concerned, that house would be reason enough to reconsider my general heterosexual proclivities, had I known she was trolling. As I'd recalled, she'd taught piano, had the charming habit of storing her unmentionables in gracefully stacked hat boxes, and she moved like Candice Bergen.

"*Oh*, Bill. Is that where you learned those amazing moves in the bedroom?"

His skills when making love were obviously coached. He knew right when to go where, when to stop, when to proceed. I'd imagined it had to do with training animals, but a lot made sense now.

"She is *waaay* out of my league. If you can land her, your future is sealed in Camelot," I said, suddenly feeling self-conscious of my misgivings.

He explained that she was now seeing a Shakespeare professor at Cal and seemed to be pretty happy. "She's okay," he assured me. "I'm focusing on you."

"Cindy Brown," I repeated, rocking my head side to side. Suddenly aware of my flaws, I lifted myself from the bed and walked into the bathroom.

"Cindy Brown" I said to my haggard reflection in the mirror.

Comparing myself to other women is a practice I disengaged from many years ago. In high school, my long-term boyfriend, Doug, had previously been dropped by Laurie Ivantosh. Laurie Ivantosh? No way. She was older than he was, with a long, willowy waist, dark hair down to her perfectly lobed breasts barely encased in her halter top. Doug had pictures of her all over the place in cut-off jeans. My obsession with her was unbearable, causing me to sit behind her parent's house with binoculars and dig through Doug's cupboards for old love letters. When I broke down sobbing while clothes-shopping with my mother because a woman who merely looked like Miss Ivantosh walked by, things changed.

"What on earth?" My mother sat me down in the ladies' lounge in Macy's department store. "You are a beautiful girl, inside and out. Doug is with you because he loves you."

The following week, I was sitting in the office of a therapist who taught me behavior modification. I was to clap my hands fiercely and shout "No!" whenever my mind drifted to comparison. Learning to understand that jealousy served no one was just one of the many strengthening tools Mother empowered me with.

There, in the bathroom, I clapped my hands.

"Is everything alright?" Bill, outside the door, was aware I'd been in the lavatory for an extended period.

I straightened my spine and opened the door, where I was greeted with a kiss. Bill was going to do whatever was right for him. Just the notion that he found me attractive made me feel fortunate. I knew Cindy was a better match for him and it would only be a matter of time. It was all part of the journey.

Bill had a plethora of good karma on his side for having taken great care of his wife. He had a lot going for him, with his gentle way of explaining his every feeling and his loving commitment to his grown daughter, who was an advocate for the Chamber of Oakland.

Within a few weeks, he sat me down to say, "I think I still have feelings for Cindy Brown."

"Okay," I whimpered.

Examining his blue, blue eyes, I committed them to memory and sewed them in my heart, as the winds of love carried him away.

Through my life he drifted, diaphanous as Peter Pan. Like so many others, I accepted the waxing and waning of all of these feelings as yet another learning experience. Like a game of rock, paper, scissors—I was practicing wins and losses at such a rapid pace that rather than experiencing pain, I felt a kind of joy that comes with the wisdom that each encounter was rare and radiant.

Not long after, I found a "like star" on OkCupid from a Shakespeare professor at Cal. He seemed interested enough to invite me to Chez Panisse in Berkeley. I love Chez Panisse for more reasons than I can list. Don seemed like an interesting and intelligent guy. We naturally spoke over our goat cheese salad about the quantum work of Shakespeare, and the genius and timeless qualities of Shakespeare's works. I knew this must be the guy that Ms. Cindy Brown had intermissioned with, so I waited for the right time to bring up the subject. I figured the after-dinner cappuccino would be a prime time.

"I know someone you know," I purred.

What a mistake.

Obviously still ensnared in the abyss created by Cindy Brown, the rest of the hour was consumed with his profound letdown from what he was sure was the woman of his dreams. The thought that they were going to get married after dating for a month seemed rather dramatic to me. He walked me to my car, with nary a hug or peck on the cheek, and continued to text me through the night, not letting up until way past midnight.

> She really let me down after I was sure we had a connection.

> She told me that we were in love and destined to be together.

> I'd waited all my life for her.

> Let it go. Bill's just a guy with a shitty house. He doesn't share his daughter at all. Cindy might just be a vixen sent on your path for a reason.

I finally turned my phone off.

The following morning, Bill called to inform me that "Shakespeare Don" had screenshot my texts and shared them with Cindy. Now why on earth Don would do such a thing is beyond bizarre.

"My house is shitty?" Bill wailed.

"Well, not really shitty. It just needs some work." My cheeks burned. I just hate it when I get caught talking behind someone's back. It is always a best practice never to do that.

"And what do you mean, I don't share my daughter? What the hell does that mean?"

"I'm sorry Bill. I guess I was trying to make him feel better."

"The guy's a lunatic."

I begged Bill to meet me for coffee, to which he begrudgingly accepted. I apologized again and he returned a vase of mine. We agreed that anyone bathing in the studies of Shakespeare would naturally be compelled to stir up dust. We found a way to laugh about the whole performance and he commended my bravery in going out with Don, even having known who he was, and for being a good sport in letting go of what I'd hoped would be my tiger.

Later, I watched Bill on Facebook traveling through Paris with his graceful cohort, Cindy Brown. All *la joie de vivre* as they toured the Marie Antoinette exhibit at the Louvre. All, as I sacrificed my heart on his happiness, exactly as it should be.

My car was in the shop for weeks after my accident. The adjuster took my statement of having turned left on a green light and covered the cost of repairs and a rental car.

"How is the woman who hit me? I trust she wasn't hurt?" I asked.

To my complete shock, my adjuster informed me that the other driver had stated that I'd run a red arrow. She only had liability coverage and her car was a total loss. In short, she was screwed.

Oh no, I thought, searching the crevices of my memory. Could I have been in the wrong? I decided to change my story to "perhaps the arrow was red." But gainsay is not accepted with insurance companies, whose main objective is saving money. As I recalled, this gal was no older than twenty. Most likely it would be impossible for her to just go out and buy another car. I remembered our hug, standing on the curb of 40th and Broadway. We hadn't even discussed fault—I thought it was hers, she'd clearly felt certain the error was mine.

"The Goddess is leading me on my journey," I explained to the befuddled adjustor. "She's allowing me to survive on nothing but grace and art. I can cover this. Please, let me do this."

I thought of Sunday, my catfisher, trapped in Nigeria, uncounted and underprivileged. I thought of my new friends that I'd been pursuing and photographing for the project. Lives and circumstances of hardship and courage that were schooling me with empathy and compassion, allowing my art to illuminate justice. I could not allow myself to be a selfish, entitled, white bitch. I simply had to make this right.

"Sorry Reenie," he confided, "it doesn't work that way."

President Trump fired James Comey on May 9, while the FBI director was in the middle of investigating whether his campaign colluded with the Russians in the election. Trump said in a meeting with Russian officials on May 10 that he fired Comey to get rid of this "Russia thing" and explained to his guests that firing that "nut job" was the right decision at the right time. The White House published Trump's first full budget report allocating $1.6 billion for a Mexican border wall and a ten percent increase in military spending. Reductions included $800 million in Medicaid, $190 million from food stamps, Meals on Wheels, and drug treatments programs, as well as the elimination of student loan subsidies. This man seemed to lack any redeeming qualities, only acting upon the most dangerous impulses.

My Summer with Dani

Things at last became impossible at the Drama Farm. Molly's prosthetic limb company asked her if she would move to San Diego, which caused her to feel anxious. With the intention of helping her decide, I booked her an Airbnb in San Diego and sleuthed out the pockets of artists' communities there for her to explore. In tandem, I contacted the head taxidermist at the Oakland Museum and asked if perhaps she had a lead on some other kind of fabrication Molly might do in order to keep her near me. In discovering the Scientific Arts studio in Richmond, I urged her to check it out, which she did, and loved it. Yet, when push came to shove, the decision became overwhelming and I found Molly in a heap on her bed, eyes darting, and her hands losing circulation. I was witnessing anxiety, personified. I felt utterly helpless and responsible for assuming she was strong enough to make a decision.

"She can't stay here," her mother explained. "I'm taking her back to Reno where I can take care of her."

Warren, as well, was spiraling. We had a dispute over money, and with no clear contract, it became evident my time remaining there was to be short-lived. Collecting images I had taken to document my season there, from Rick dying, my catfisher, Molly's fragility, young Sashy, and the garden, I created a slideshow to express my feelings. I set it to an eerie Pat Metheny tune sung in Russian to narrate the strangeness of the whole experience. As if to say, with love: "I don't really understand these words, I don't really understand this thing, but it was real."

I felt certain I would never see any of these people again. It was the child who was the hardest to leave.

My friend, Jim Cooper, the contractor who had helped me transform Scoundrel's kitchen and living room two years earlier, serendipitously asked if I might know someone to sublet his home. Having built a place on the river in Idaho, he wanted to experiment with retirement and see if he could live solely up there for several months. That someone he was looking for would be me, although I knew the sublet rent would be too steep.

I reached out to my old high school friend, Dani, and let her know I'd secured a place for the two of us, in the hopes this union could work. It had been such a lovely coincidence that we had found ourselves single at the same time, in this later stage of life, and had been walking and dining frequently to share our free-falling life experiences. A communications professional and lobbyist, Dani had just finished a term working for a state assemblywoman, and was hoping to either advocate for the Wine and Farm bureau in Napa, work for a large developer in Walnut Creek, or, what I was praying for, be hired as a strategist for the Mayor of Oakland, Libby Schaaf.

"If I don't land any work, I'm planning on jettisoning on a jaunt through Europe alone. If I get the Oakland job, sure, I'd love to live with you."

Two weeks later, she called me from Prague. "I've landed a job advocating for a company in Oakland!"

I picked her up at the airport and brought her back to her new temporary home with me.

Living with Dani was like fresh, organic cream. The picket-fenced bungalow situated in the sleepy, postwar Glenview district of Oakland was just our size. Deciduous trees of maple, pistachio, and pecan transformed to reflect the seasons where children chortled on their scooters through the garden-lined sidewalks. A galley kitchen, perpetually glowing fireplace, a resting room, office, and two perfectly sized tandem bedrooms served us nicely. Both of our rooms opened to the backyard, where I promptly strung carnival lights in the giant Keebler Elf walnut tree. I planted flowers from seed and spread a tablecloth on the outdoor table.

"We could have nice dinner parties out here," I said, as I brought throw pillows out of my room and fluffed them on the picnic bench. "Maybe even house concerts. I'm eager to entertain, now that we have a place of our own. The feeling here is quite salubrious. Would you take a look at that wisteria!"

Salubrious is not a word that I'd made up. I had gleaned it from my Merriam Webster word-of-the-day email notifications. *Salubrious*: health-giving, beneficial. Wanting to fill this chapter of my life with just that, I'd taken up flute lessons and begun practicing William Tell's Overture daily.

"Whatever you want, Reen. As long as you cook."

"I've got it!" I chirped with a spin. "Salubrious Sunday. Twelve of our favorite people, a different group every time. The best goddamn meal I can muster, and everyone must bring a song, story, or anecdote. Do you like it?"

"I love it."

Perhaps due to her skill as an advocate, it seemed every single thing that came out of Dani's mouth was an affirmation. She would announce what she was doing in the moment and her future plans for the day, the week, her life. "I'm going to make a spinach, protein, chocolate shake for us now. How 'bout I set this here? I have noticed the way you arranged these flowers. Come and let me show you what is interesting to me, now. I will be hiking with friends 'til noon tomorrow."

Most mornings began with Lily Allen music erupting from our Alexa machine, singing "Fuck You (Very Much)," to which we would dance around the house in bath towels in reaction to the latest Trump atrocities.

Much of Dani's time was spent in Jim's office on the phone where I overheard shockingly enormous deals going down. With her gentle hand and carefully crafted connections, she smoothed out alliances with cannabis farms and city officials, water companies and oil manufacturers. This glorious, grown-up girlfriend from my pubescent chapters of hijinks, where we orchestrated the senior class sleep-over on the front lawn at school and *psilocybinned* throughout our formative years, had flourished into a woman with nerves of steel. Though strong, she was also capable of sharing her deepest fears and emotional landmines with dewy eyes.

Communication was our art project. It seemed all was possible for this sweet, open book, and her emotional intelligence filled me with a sense of solid sisterhood that delighted me day after day. Like a pair of well-worn jeans, she fit me comfortably—our hearts weaving together a strong, feminine shawl to protect us.

"I'll drop a pin on my phone map when I get there so you can know where I was last," she joked, as she glided out of the house in the highest heels and shortest skirt I had seen her in. Off to a party as the plus-one of a political official; her company had sent her there to find out why Alvin Solesto hadn't paid his $200,000 invoice. I looked up the man via Google to find the face of an obvious mobster, a terrifying character somehow acquitted of killing a man with his bare hands. How does one do that?

"Exactly what do you do, Dani?" I asked her when she at last got home, after worrying about her all evening.

"I help people communicate effectively and clearly."

"Does the skirt help?"

We tried to remember where Jim's things had been as we replaced all of his hunting/fishing Republican art with women's art. I phoned the Snake Boyz requesting that I come get my collection of wall art and photographs from my house to put up at Jim's sublet.

"No!" my tenant, Vinnie, wailed. "These photos are the soul of your house and they must stay here!"

Naturally, it was inappropriate for him to call my photos a fixture, yet in a way they were, and I was reminded that my home up there was intact, strong, and waiting, waiting for me. Waiting for me to solve this mystery of love and find a partner to call my own. Someone to take care of me and help me get back to my home.

"Okay, Vinnie," I conceded. "Just leave everything where it is. I'll create a different art-scape for Dani and my current domicile."

I decided the theme would be "women of any era," and nothing was to cost more than sixty dollars. Sifting through junk shops and garage sales, I collected some thought-provoking gems. A gigantic Renoir replica of a sultry French woman contemplating the river's edge, a *cheruby*-round oil painting starkly revealing the graceful curve of a woman's bottom, a giant bronze statue of a female troubadour, guitar strapped on her back. I met a fellow at a street fair that specialized in old negatives recovered from abandoned storage spaces. He conjured for me two great treasures. Two young women in the 1920s in full-on, flapper regalia, clinging to each other in what appeared to be a trash heap, and three naked 1950s girls playing volleyball on the beach. At one Salubrious Sunday celebration, Dani's nineteen-year-old son emerged from the bathroom, blushing.

"There is porn in your bathroom, Mom."

"Get used to it," Dani laughed. "Reenie is edgy."

Hairy Vaj, Please

It was a sunny June morning when I was sitting up in my bed, journaling my morning pages, as prescribed by the book, *The Artist's Way*. As this prescription aligned with other systems, my sister's "Love Breakthrough" gurus, the general "Law of Attraction" guidelines, *The Tao of Dating*, and whatever strong Goddess power guiding me, my writing was in full thrust. While writing, I allow myself to stray as necessary: walk around the yard, smoke a cigarette, and return to my down comforter and laptop.

Settling back into my soft bed, I opted to do a little phone media. I opened Facebook. Apparently, many friends were enjoying the outdoors, posting images of flower gardens or lanky children in togas and tasseled oxford caps, holding up diplomas. School was recently on break, and families were together and out, all over the country.

Clicking on the familiar image of Scoundrel embracing his dog, I enjoyed a five-minute video of him in Palm Springs. He appeared to be waterskiing ... no ... skateboarding behind a golf cart via rope tow.

Apparently, someone in the golf cart—probably Mortgage Broker or some other scantily clad stranger—was holding the recording device. The clip was jagged and jerky with laughter. The rope, appearing to be a good ten yards behind the vehicle, slacked and tightened as Mike slalomed through a palm-tree-lined neighborhood, cocktail, complete with drink umbrella, balanced in one hand. "Faster," he indicated with a thumbs-up, as he crouched low on his skateboard, lifting his big toe and leaning back to take in more speed. His mouth was agape with pleasure, exposing almost all of his perfect white teeth. I closed my eyes, anticipating a crash, remembering so well that fear, and chuckled.

I clicked over to my OkCupid site and shuffled through the river of changing faces. Given my experience, I could now swipe rather rapidly. The vast majority of these men were abominable, if not ghastly. Yet, I'd vowed not to consider this practice a waste of time, but rather, a study of sorts. Strange as they may be, these men were my species and this was a chapter of my life I was trying to understand. As Walt Whitman reminded me, I was discovering myself in dissimilar fellows.

"Oh, my God!" I shouted.

Dani and I were aware we'd been working in tandem for some hours. We'd opted to give each other space to work or create from our prospective rooms.

"What now?" Dani shouted through the walls from her room. "May I make you a shake? I can do banana and kale, with black cherries and chocolate protein."

"That would be dreamy. Then you *must* see this."

I listened to the *tss, tss, tss,* of Dani's fuzzy slippers in the kitchen orchestrating her ritual shake. I loved that she took care of me, ensuring I secured all of my daily requirements in one brown, goopy glass.

"Here," she said, handing me my tall glass of morning elixir. Opening the covers of my bed, she slid herself beside me. "What's up. Are you writing?"

"First, look at this." I showed her the video of Scoundrel, which she watched with determined eyes. "You just can't make this shit up," I said. "Everything he does is just so *him*."

"I'm so glad that's over, Reen. You are over him, right?"

"I am, Dani." I said, looking down at my phone.

"Then why do you even follow him? He's a reckless fool. He's reckless with life, he was reckless with your heart."

"I'm in control of what happens to me. I don't want to forget anything, Dan. That's why I write. He's a part of my story. Now, look at this."

Opening the OkCupid app, I showed Dani where I'd left the page open to a particular profile with the handle, "HairyVajPlease." In his profile picture, this guy was completely naked, straddling a piece of raw wood, knees drawn up to his chest, in what appeared to be an abandoned gun battery like those at the forts in the Presidio. He held in his hand a large piece of plywood that he seemed to be reading like Moses would his scroll of commandments. He, the plywood, and his surroundings were splattered with house paint like a Jackson Pollock piece. This blonde, covered with tattoos and a full, scruffy beard, described himself as forty-two and living in San Francisco, and he had a twenty-three-percent match rate with me. That's beyond low.

"What the fuck is the matter with these people? Reen, you worry about where my work takes me. If you think I'm going to let you go out with this lunatic, you've got another thing coming." Dani snickered.

I had pushed off the down coverlet and was now rolling with laughter on the edge of the bed, punching the pillow in hysteria. "I'm gonna pee my pants!" I stumbled as I guffawed into the bathroom.

As I stood to flush, my eyes flashed on one of our newest wall acquisitions. The old black-and-white photograph of three gals playing volleyball on the beach. With photographs, it's always important to re-examine them frequently. Every time you study art, like the face of a flower, you will notice something new. Like a garden or a child, like life, change is constantly emerging.

Dani entered the open-doored bathroom, still in need of an answer. "Reen, you are not going out with this guy, right?"

My gaze lingered on the beach-volleyball image, examining the faces of the subjects. Probably in their early twenties, one had long hair to her waist, another a short blonde bob and horn-rimmed glasses. The kind of girl you'd be more likely see at church than naked holding a volleyball over her head, yet I noticed a tiny star tattooed on her hip. The photo was old, weird, and wonderful. Like *The Three Graces*, it was certainly set up, but by whom? I swept over the timeless piece, following the line down past pouty breasts and supple hips of youth. My eyes rested on the patches between their legs. All three of them donned a significantly piliferous bush.

"Noreen!" Dani now used my given name, reminding me that she'd known me longer than many, and had the power to discipline the child in me. "What's going on in that brain of yours?" She followed me as I walked through the house to re-examine all the art we had amassed.

"I wonder, Dan," I started, sitting down now on our soft leather sofa. "I've never asked. Do you shave your vagina?"

"Yes, all of it."

"Why?"

"The cowboy likes it that way. I don't think you should answer this guy's profile, Reen. He scares me."

"I won't," I assured her. "It just brings up an interesting subject in my study of men, women, femininity, power, and prowess. I think I'm going to start asking."

"Sounds interesting." Dani's eyes met mine with her usual unconditional love and unperforated faith.

She had a way of lowering her chin when she smiled to remind me of all of the secrets we shared. I'd been loving those green eyes on and off for forty years. We'd been each other's cheerleaders through all kinds of changes, from sex and drugs to husbands and children.

"Never leave me, Dan. Your support means so much to me." I fondled my flute, which I left out to remind me to practice.

"Never."

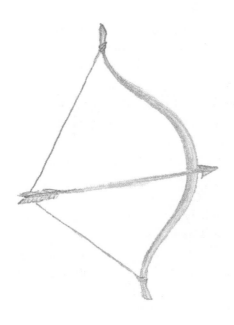

Clayton

Clayton was a ceramicist and a design instructor. He asked if I would like to come to his studio in Jingletown and see some of his work. Jingletown, a burrow in Oakland, used to be called "the ghetto." It was still knee-deep in garbage and homeless encampments, yet artists loved the region, as a Quonset hut, crane bay, or wool mill could make for a groovy workspace. Old toilets, washing machines, and car parts constituted great flowerpots. Opinions were expressed in gigantic mosaic displays everywhere, and, with some reinforcement, nearly any piece of garbage could make a pretty good garden chair.

Much more interesting when kinetic than in his profile picture, Clayton was tall, and donned suspenders and a Harrison-Ford-a-la-Indiana-Jones fedora. His work was huge and beautiful and exuded a feminine wisdom, which I later discovered came from his time with his men's group. He enjoyed performing pagan rituals high on mountaintops at dawn, praying in the sun with little wands and bags of stones. I took him to the Hardly Strictly Bluegrass festival, where Patty Griffin sang "Making Pies," and, as providence would have it, we ran into Rand, whom Clayton had known from the men's group. I explained to Clayton about my experience with Rand, and how sometimes men just disappear like a fellow driver might on the freeway.

"I'm not one of those," Clayton explained. "I thought his name was Randy."

The next week, Clayton showed up with some quivers and bows and took me to the archery range up near Scoundrel's house. As the movie re-release of *Wonder Woman* was still fueling the flames of femininity, I felt like a warrior clutching this compound bow in my cutoff jeans. I went into the closet at my photo studio and dug up an artful Goddess crown and took to wearing it in public again.

"Where the hell did you get that?" said Scoundrel, as he came into the shop and noticed my headpiece.

"It makes me feel powerful," I said.

"Let me guess, you're dating a wizard now?"

I thought about it for a minute. "Well, I guess I kind of am."

Mike could have a way of making me feel small, a feeling I avoided when possible. It would be foreign for him to feel compassion for me and my faith in destiny and headpieces.

"Look at this!" He held up a plain, white piece of paper lined with bullet points of the things on his to-do list. He always drew little squares in front of his lists, so he could check off things as they happened.

☐ Tom Petty
☐ Alan Parsons Project
☐ Lucinda Williams
☐ Clean girlfriend's rain gutters
☐ Thirsty Thursday
☐ The English Beat
☐ Oakland Raiders game
☐ Paul Simon

I remembered this man of few responsibilities and misgivings. Changing his day T-shirt to dressy button-ups in the evening to go to expensive concerts, sometimes more than three a month. I'd enjoyed the previous concerts and the flashy restaurants in my tawdry clothes of his choice. I just had to remind myself that it was never truly me. In truth, I was still trying to find me.

"How great." I smiled. "You look great, babe. I loved the piece on Facebook of you skateboarding behind the golf cart."

"I was so buzzed!" he sputtered. "I almost died."

"That will never happen, Mike."

"Are you going out with Clayton?" Dani asked that evening.

"Yes, we're going to dinner and a movie."

"You don't seem very excited about him. He's a very sweet man, Reen."

"I haven't really decided how I feel. He seems to be coming on kind of strong."

That evening, Clayton came over with some of his art as a gift for Dani and me. Two matching coffee mugs and an orchid pot. The beauty of his ceramic work reminded me of a grandmother's quilt—a blue-and-gray Raku glaze with perfectly imperfect hand grooves down the sides.

"These are priceless," I said, while cradling and caressing my mug, running my finger down each groove.

"You are priceless," he grinned, enfolding me a bit too hard, bringing his face too close to mine. "And I am in love with you."

Dani flashed an expression of concern my way, then quickly reverted to a smile for Clayton's exchange with her.

Later that evening, Dani reinforced that I was required to be honest with Clayton. She knew me too well. "You date like a squirrel eats sunflower seeds, looking for Mister Right. Clayton is not him."

"But he's such a great, solid guy. Why can't I make myself more attracted to him? It's just not fair."

I enjoyed the attention of Clayton. I enjoyed having something to do with someone, but something simply wasn't right. The animal magnetism didn't tug at me. There are more important things to consider in a partner than sex, but I couldn't make myself feel drawn. I didn't dive at the phone when he called.

After sending me countless invitations to events, with my responses being that I was always busy that night, Clayton suddenly dropped off. "Oh, man," I thought, "I have hurt him."

Dani frothed milk to cover my morning coffee. "Chocolate in mine!" she'd chirp, as she set the two mugs in front of her. "This mug is mine. I know it because it has this flaw in it right here. I just love these. Clayton is so talented!"

I would sit in my bed, mug in hand, and feel guilty, shitty, and lonely. A lesson in clarity. I often thought I should just call Clayton and see how he was doing, but where would the conversation go? I'd essentially ghosted him. I felt shame.

Many months later, New Year's Eve to be exact, Clayton sent me a graphic of light pouring out of hands into the universe with an apology:

> I'm sorry I disappeared, but I fell in love with another. I've been feeling poorly for months because I hadn't been clear with you.

"Oh, Dani, look!" I showed her. "Isn't it ridiculous how much worry we could have spared each other?"

"Sometimes the Universe takes care of things for us," she said.

I took my tiny clippers, trimmed my orchid sitting in Clayton's hand-made pot, and moved it to a sunnier spot. With a smile, I breathed, "Thank you, Clayton."

MILF

If I were to have the fortuitous luck to have Ann-Margret land at my table for breakfast, this is how it would go. Candace, a friend of Scoundrel's, was, at most, a contemporary of mine. I had met her at a political rally for the mayor of Oakland, Libby Schaaf. Candace's beauty was movie-star-league, and I found myself looking at her from several angles for mere pleasure.

Standing near six-feet-tall, her hourglass figure was designed to fill out a short-sleeved cashmere exactly as it was intended. Her unruly blonde bangs, purposefully cut too short, created a heart-shaped curl at the center of her forehead, which pointed to her piercing green eyes that seemed to have more moisture than the rest of ours. They literally sparkled.

I invited Candace to breakfast so she could explain the images she'd been flailing at me via text. She wanted to make me feel better about the loss of Scoundrel and let me know that there were plenty of fish in the sea. The types of men she was dating were deliciously disgraceful.

> This is Glen. He's a pro
> baseball player.

I'd received her text while lacing up my sneakers for a walk. Nothing could prepare me for the images that followed. I suppose the operative word would be young, I mean *young*.

Most of the time, men of color, all of the time, close to naked, the boys Candice was fraternizing with were surreal. Like carved marble, these glistening men exposed abdomens too dangerous to ski down. Glaring into the camera with a look of violent hunger, I just had to know what was going on here.

> Carl is a drug dealer. He
> likes to fuck in the car.

> Oh My God.

What I knew of Candace was her success in a beauty care company she had created, and her long and seemingly endless divorce. We saw each other at conspicuous events, like awards ceremonies and press parties for celebrities that she always somehow attended for free. She would approach me with strong drinks she'd pilfered from some handsome drifter and bump me with her shoulder.

"Come sit by me," she'd purr. "What's the deal with Scoundrel? Why would he leave you for that troll? You know you can do better than that! I've got tickets for an after-party at Paul Simon's show at the Paramount. Do you want to go?"

For fear of ending up somewhere dangerous, I always found a way to separate from her at these public events, yet these recent disturbing images needed explanation.

Now, in the loud breakfast joint, I watched Candace scrape the filling out of her quiche to avoid the carbohydrates associated with the crust.

"I'm worried that you are putting yourself in danger, darling. Are you feeling loved by these men?" I lowered my voice and leaned in toward her to avoid disturbing the families with young children surrounding us.

"These guys like me because they consider me a MILF."

"A MILF?"

"Mother I'd Like to Fuck. I am a fantasy to these boys. They will do whatever I ask of them . . . and I mean, whatever."

"And what do you want from them?" I fidgeted in my chair, trying to appear like we were having a conversation about work or house paint.

"I sometimes like to tie them up and tease them. I like to be begged for sex. When men are powerless, I get really turned on." Her eyes flashed a crazed expression.

"Good God, Candace," I practically shouted my whisper. "Now, *that* seems dangerous!"

Candace threw her head back, barely withholding a squeal. "It's fun. You know, the sky's the limit."

"The sky's the limit," I speculated. "I guess none of these guys are marriage material. Do you ever think about finding a secure partner?"

"I don't want security. I don't want love." Candace's eyes fixed on me. "I want power. I've been hurt too many times. I will not be hurt again."

On June 1, President Trump announced his intent to withdraw the US from the 2015 Paris climate agreement, prompting criticism from world leaders. Tesla's Elon Musk and then-Disney CEO Bob Iger resigned from the President's business advisory council in protest. Later, Trump hosted a luncheon at the White House with Republican senators to discuss repealing the Affordable Care Act.

Almost two hundred Congressional Democrats filed lawsuits against President Trump, alleging violation of the Foreign Emoluments Clause that prohibits granting nobility and receiving gifts.

Attorney General Jeff Sessions testified to the Senate Intelligence Committee on matters related to alleged Russian interference in Trump's election.

James Comey testified to the Senate Intelligence Committee in an open hearing in which he reiterated his statement that President Trump was not under investigation by the FBI during his tenure, but he did not explicitly confirm whether or not he considered the President to have obstructed any investigation. Trump accused him of lying under oath.

I was still on the journey to find that true love to care for me.

A Purse Named Bonnie

I have a purse named Bonnie. One of those stiff, rawhide cowboy numbers from the '70s with the heat-tooled florets and lettering. Above the florets, in a *ranchy* font, brags the name of whomever had the purse customized at the county fair—obviously, Bonnie. At some point, Bonnie tired of it and discarded it for a donation pile. The gentle ladies at Goodwill cleaned it up, and when I saw it, I wanted it. I transferred my keys, calling-card case, hairbrush, wallet, mints, and three lip colors into it, and carried something new for a while.

When transferring to a new purse, we do it hastily, always leaving something behind in the one destined to live in the fallow pasture of the closet—lip balms, stray mints, hair bands, and bobby pins. One day we'll return to the old Coach bag that will never wear out and hopefully find a few twenties or a memorable ticket stub and decide then to turn it upside down, throw out the debris, and start over. I thought it to be wildly serendipitous that I'd opted for a purse-over the day before I'd met Dick, since his wife's name was Bonnie.

Dick's profile picture looked alluring to me with his regal frame in a golf cart. His handle was "Eric," and when I beckoned his call he told me he was married, which does not fit in the parameters of my dating criteria.

I'm window shopping.

Guys married for a long time sometimes troll for adventure. I decided I would, for interest's sake, talk him off the ledge of infidelity. To have a long and happy marriage is an elusive and pure thing, something my folks and their folks before them had embraced. I like to believe that I know the recipe for success, which is ludicrous as a woman twice-divorced.

When I learned more about him, eventually prying out his real name, I found, with very little effort online, that he was not only married, but was a pastor at a church on the "posh" side of town. The best way to investigate him thoroughly would be to go to his church and witness his exhortation.

In my blue-polka-dot, floor-length dress, cowboy boots, and powder-blue beret, after donning Bonnie, my purse, I sat in the front pew of the congregation and swayed to Dick's rock-and-roll religion.

I love church. It is my fabric, a certain sunlight on a distant *déjà vu* haunts me on Sunday mornings, as I have let the ritual evaporate, yet here, I didn't recognize the music. Where were the old hymns that I knew by heart: "The Old Rugged Cross" and "How Great Thou Art?" I couldn't sing to these modern songs played by a full-piece, electric-guitar band. After the service, I followed the others through the receiving line and met Bonnie, as well as Dick's pregnant daughter.

"My third," she blushed. These women were pure and beautiful with soft white hands tipped with long red nails. They both wore huge, recently polished diamond rings displaying their devotion. Dick held my handshake a bit too long and bore into my eyes.

"Welcome. I'm glad you came. What brought you?"

"I'm window-shopping." I pulled my hand out of his with such ferocity that I almost lost my balance on my slippery cowboy boots. He gave me a classic, *clergic* smile.

Lingering for a while on the patio with the unfamiliar coffee congregation, I remembered these same such events from my youth. Skipping around in my Mary Janes with the other kids. Diving for the cookies or cake on the paper doilies next to the percolator and powdered Coffee-Mate creamer. Mother had cherished her bond with her friends of faith. The *après-caucus* was almost as important as the minister's sermon, which she listened to intently, often taking notes on her program. I was there for the music, the Certs that Mom would slip me, and the benediction, which inferred the service was close to over.

"Go now," the pastor would say. "Go now in peace. Go now in courage. Go now in thanks. Go now in one body."

I felt like a little soldier making a promise so I could finally go now, outside to play.

Admiring a little girl of about four or five in her summer dress, I felt a warm breath behind me.

"You're ten times prettier in person than your photos online."

I froze. Just then, the little girl I'd been studying ran full speed toward us. Dick lowered himself into an instinctive crouch and swooped her up, spinning around twice, her ankles in flight.

"My grandchild, Chelsey!" he beamed.

At last, something normal.

"Hi Chelsey. I'm Reenie," I chirped, and thought to myself, "I hope we never, ever meet again."

I let him have it when I got home.

> What the fuck are you thinking? You have an empire. Your family is radiant. Hundreds of people look to you for guidance. You're a fool. Let's have a picnic.

Dick met me on the grassy shores of Lake Merritt, where I laid out my usual fare: cheese, pate, oysters, an artichoke. I was practicing guitar when he showed up.

"What did you think of the service?" he asked, easily tumbling down to sit next to me on the flowery blanket I'd laid out. For some reason, I felt like I'd known this man for a very long time.

I started a new song, guessing at the chords and sang.

"Blessed assurance, Jesus is mine. Oh, what a foretaste of glory divine. Heir of salvation. Purchase of God. Born of his spirit. Washed in his blood."

Dick joined in the chorus.

"This is my story, this is my song, praising my Savior, all the day long. This is my story, this is my song, praising my Savior, all the day long."

"Impressive," he smirked.

"A family favorite. Why don't you incorporate some of the good ol' songs? I miss them. That would really be the reason I would go to church more regularly."

"You didn't like the music?" He stretched himself long beside me, observing the food I had laid out. "Wow, this is awfully nice of you. I feel honored."

Picking up a white cloth napkin embroidered with purple pansies, he observed it closely, then brought it to his nose and closed his eyes. This gave me the opportunity to look at him more closely.

He was indeed quite handsome in a Paul Newman kind of way. Tall, nearly lanky, with broad shoulders that I fancied lying in. His temples were beginning to grey from many years of thick, light-brown curls. He smelled good. Really good.

"I'm in my fifties, Dick. I'm nostalgic. I understand you needing to bring in the younger crowd, but it's hard to sing rock and roll. How did you decide on this path?"

Pulling off a slice of baguette and slathering it with pate, he took a bite. His eyes widened with pleasure. "I always knew God had a plan for me and I loved religious studies. I'm a story guy. I think I tell a good story."

He picked up my guitar and started playing a Latin flamenco piece. "Oh God, he plays well, too," I thought.

"What stories are you telling your beautiful wife, Bonnie?" I said, pulling off my boots to enjoy the grass.

"I'll never betray Bonnie. She is a great woman."

"Well, that's a relief. You know if you lost that congregation over adultery, you'd never forgive yourself."

We steered the conversation to biblical adventures and parables, and after two hours flew by, he stood up, wiping the grass off of his trousers. "I'll need to go now. I cannot thank you enough for such a splendid afternoon."

I stood to walk him to his car, which was parked not far from our picnic. He fumbled with his keys, and I wondered if I shouldn't have stayed with the picnic and just waved him goodbye. I had no intention of giving him any ideas.

His kiss was sudden, desperate, long, and deep. At first resisting, I fell limp into it, as if neither of us had any regulation. When at last we came up for air, I lay my head on his strong shoulder and gave him an assuring hug. I felt a soft, human connection with his soul.

"This will not happen, Dick. Nothing good could come from this. You can call me anytime, but this relationship will not be one of dishonesty. I will be your friend. We can keep it a secret, but I will never kiss you again."

Dick tightened his hug, allowing us a moment to exhale together, then releasing me, lifted my chin with his thumb.

"Thank you," he said, with his ecclesiastical grin.

I walked back to the picnic and began packing it up. I wondered about Dick and what it would be like to have his life. He was the shepherd of his flock. Did he feel suppressed, or did he have some bad-boy craving to have an affair. Well, whatever the situation, I stood to gain absolutely nothing here, I resolved.

Dick did call again, countless times. Usually late at night from his screened-in porch in the warm valley. I pictured him drinking scotch, smoking cigars, surrounded by colorful plastic toys from the churchy activities of his family life. He would tell me about the day's events, the Rice Krispie treats Bonnie had made, the nativity pageant plans, and the growing babies. Sometimes we would work together on sermon ideas for hours. He would often tell me I was beautiful and how he longed to touch me, comments I would redirect. There was something extremely vulnerable about this monarch, and I continued the relationship because I felt I was, in some way, supporting him. For many months, I was his platonic Scheherazade, protecting myself and him from sabotage.

"Perhaps you were meant to be a Mormon," I whispered into my phone late one rainy evening. "Then you could have several wives."

"I don't believe in polygamy. It's wrong."

"Polyamory is all around us, Dick. It would just have to be all right with your wife."

"Would you like that, Reenie?"

"I would not at all. I am looking for one true love. I'm also trying to convince you that you have already found your one true love."

Eventually, Dick faded away and other events filled my time. It was perhaps a year later that I heard his church had folded, and that Bonnie had left him.

What had formed this man's ambitions and appetite? Could something have been different that might have made him feel more secure and satisfied in his marriage? I wondered if Bonnie shaved her nethers?

Did he assume that sinners had a happier life than saints? Truth be told, there is no supreme, unadulterated purity available to us. All we can strive for is authenticity. I wanted this so badly for Dick.

"What a jerk," Dani and other friends decided of Dick, as they had before, of Sunday, the catfisher.

But "jerk" was the wrong word for Dick. He was a kind and intelligent man. His window to the divine was magnetic to women, and the power he felt was intoxicating. He was a boy, wanting attention for his prowess.

I searched my heart again, and came up with the same flimsy resolve. "Look with compassion."

Little Angels Everywhere

Things I hate: peeling garlic, putting a cold, wet swimsuit on a dry body, dogs that don't come when they're called, applying mascara, and driving.

I cannot discern why it is legal to drive at the speeds we do, particularly when it is raining. Having been pulled over three times by the CHP for suspected drunk driving when I was merely driving too slowly is one of my children's greatest, tell-it-again, roll-on-the-floor jokes. When going anywhere with my kids, one of them always instinctively takes the driver's seat. Changing lanes on the freeway feels to me like crossing the wake while waterskiing, and I'm not very good at that, either. Why I am alone in my absolute belief that driving is a loaded gun to the head is beyond my comprehension.

Unfortunately, driving is unavoidable in my world. I am eternally grateful for Scoundrel having leased me a comfortable and reliable vehicle that talks to me, gives me directions, and plays soothing French music. In my work as a photographer, I can abstain from commuting with rush-hour traffic and freeway imbeciles, as my studio is close by in our sleepy village. However, there is just one thing that renounces this anxiety, and I don't know why that is. When I get the call to drive to the hospital to photograph a baby dying, all fear dissipates.

It started like this. One of my clients years back had wished her third child to be a girl. Caryl and Ted had already sired two healthy little boys. Her doctor suggested they spin Ted's sperm for a girl. Apparently girl sperm is slower than boy sperm and by spinning, you can scoop out the microscopic tadpoles in the middle of the dish, thus increasing your chances of a filly. Naturally, she became pregnant with not one, but twin boys.

Being the good sport that Caryl was, she called me and asked if I would do a documentary piece about her pregnancy. I followed her gigantic tummy everywhere, using natural light and black-and-white film. I shot her and Ted playing with the kids in the house, her yummy tummy naked in the garden, family pillow fights, and trips to the doctor's office. It was during one of these sonograms that we discovered at just shy of twenty-eight weeks, one of her fetal babies had died.

"Should we continue shooting or do you want me to go away?" I asked with wet eyes.

Needless to say, this was devastating for all, and without knowing the cause of death, there could be additional heartbreak ahead. It was too soon to attempt delivery, as the one remaining child was not yet viable.

"I don't want you to go away," Caryl lifted her chin. "I want you to be at the birth. I want as much information recorded as possible for my living son."

My usually uncomplicated friend transformed into a pillar of bravery and deep substance as we waited the necessary weeks to induce. Caryl's greatest joy and greatest sorrow living like a yin and yang in her core.

To her credit, Caryl had Ted. When I refer to GWGDs (Guys With Great Dads), Ted pretty much fit the suit. He was strong, funny, and reliable.

My daughter once asked, "Why didn't you marry Ted?"

To which I plainly responded, "Because Caryl did."

When the babies were born, like all births (and deaths), the world cracked open again to reveal God's light. It was stunning. I captured beautiful images, which we sealed in a box for later.

"One in our hearts, One in our hands," the birth announcement poignantly read: "Shaw and Tate."

Another pearl was dropped on me when I found in Grandma's things an eight-by-ten, fiber-based, black-and-white photo of a tiny baby in a coffin, surrounded by flowers.

"Oh, that would be William," my aunt said plainly. "Mom and Dad were in Alaska in the thirties, and couldn't get to a hospital."

The image was dog-eared, faded, well-worn. My veritably young and innocent grandmother had used this image as a means to bereave the loss of her first born. She must have been devastated. To plunge into and through her grief, she used a photograph as a tool.

When I heard of the organization, Now I Lay Me Down to Sleep, I was all over it. I auditioned and was accepted to be that angel to help grieving mothers and fathers.

I take very seriously this volunteer work. When I get the call, all things are dropped, and I load up my camera bag. It's always sad, yet always undeniably palpable. I never see these people again after I link them to a slideshow created for them to use as a grieving tool. I fancy myself the woman with the casserole. Well-rehearsed in a situation unprecedented to them, I know what to expect, how to approach it, and what I can do.

Perhaps the fear of driving dissipates, because the work minimizes my worry in the face of service. Whatever it is, the feeling brings me close to the divine.

Once a woman lost a twin, like Caryl had. Holding her living newborn daughter, she asked me, "What do I tell her?"

It's not my job to further a relationship with these families, but in this case, I said, "May I get back to you on that?"

Caryl and Ted's youngest son would be seven by then. I had never asked, so I called Caryl.

"What did you tell him?"

"Oh, Reen. It was never a secret. Tate is the fastest skier and the best at math because he has an angel with him all the time. He keeps the pictures in his room as a reminder. They actually talk to each other. Oh, and

Reenie, please don't ever stop doing the work you do. It's more important than you can know."

"Grief and gratitude live in the same house," a dear friend had once told me.

I like that.

Similar to the songs that soothed me in Ireland months back, allowing me to really listen to stories and to try to understand "we" as a big family of people enduring tragedies and victories fills the artist in me.

Craig

Craig lived in a gated community in Marin. His profile showed him to be a handsome African American with some stature. He was forty-two, my sweet spot, and was working for NPR producing a broadcast radio show. It was important for him to talk on the phone, rather than text, which I felt to be a good sign. He worked very hard from 7:00 a.m. to 9:00 p.m. on various things, such as learning and teaching something-or-other. I looked forward to finding a time after nine when he was free to talk. From our late-night dialogue, he seemed well-educated and driven.

"I put myself through high school, college, and my master's. Now I'm in broadcasting."

Feeling interested, I asked when we might meet. Finding that time was elusive.

"As soon as I am able," he had said on two separate phone calls. I always have my catfisher radar on, but I figured I could wait a week or so.

He came across as genuine, and getting to know him a little better first felt comfortable to me. We spoke again. He had settled in after a long day.

"I rise early at seven for breakfast. After that, I stay busy all day working, exercising, taking classes, teaching some. We try to stay active."

His routine conveyed health of body and mind. I wondered if maybe he was following the practices of *The Artist's Way*.

"We? Tell me about your family."

He explained with his caressing voice that he was born in the Watts neighborhood of Los Angeles. He didn't do particularly well with his mother, and spent most of his time in and out of the foster care system.

"When I was seventeen, there was an incident in a Shakey's Pizza parking lot with a gun, and a boy passed away."

"Passed away? What does that mean?"

"He died. It happened pretty quickly."

He went on to tell me that his gated community was in Larkspur, and he was watched over very carefully, and had been for twenty years. When NPR came in to interview the inmates, Craig had come up with the idea for a regular show, "Stand Up San Quentin."

"It was so successful that they installed a studio inside for me to run."

Inside?

"Okay, wait, let me get this straight. You are incarcerated? Are you in San Quentin?"

"I will understand if you don't want to talk to me anymore," he skulked.

Twenty years in the hole was not a catastrophe but rather had been a saving grace for Craig.

"Nothing would have happened to me but the grave down there. Here, I got a new lease on life."

"You are in prison? You killed a man?"

I had so many questions. How did he get a cell phone? How did he manage a profile on OkCupid? What does it smell like? Is it cold in there? Had he ever been hurt, beaten-up, raped?

"I will understand if you don't want to talk to me anymore," he repeated.

"No, I do want to talk with you." I wanted to learn more about him. Quite frankly, he was in a better place than many men I had been dating. He was healthy, clear, and on track with his life.

He'd be out in a year and had secured employment with our local KQED station upon his remission. We spoke of possibilities of me coming in to do an interview with my camera. He snail-mailed me an application to come visit.

"Gated community!" Dani roared when I told her what I'd discovered. "That is just rich. Are you up for conjugal visits?"

"I'm just curious, Dani. What might it be like to know more closely a person who had been incarcerated for twenty years? He's probably never experienced traffic or twitter. When he gets out, he'll be a baby."

Providentially, my Rotary Club hosted a spokesperson from San Quentin two weeks later. I couldn't believe it. It was undeniable that this was the Goddess at work. Riveted to the podium, I listened to the speaker explain the innovations and activities happening on the inside.

"Could we get the lights turned off, now?" he said, as a video cued up on the giant screen in the front of the grand room.

The title was bold: "Stand Up San Quentin."

"Oh, my God," I thought.

There stood Craig. Lanky, confident, and double-dipped dark-skinned. He introduced his production by the San Quentin Media Group. My heart mollified as I listened to the stories and comedy acts of real and complex men who had made mistakes. Through performance and art, allowing themselves to be vulnerable, they were breaking down barriers through exposing grief and grace. It was spellbinding.

I called Craig that evening at the usual hour after 9:00 p.m. "I am so proud of you."

He seemed happy to hear from me.

We chatted further about me coming to visit and do a photo piece on him, but the red tape and paperwork involved, as it would be with most government entities, became too taxing. He began talking about a relationship once he was released. I knew that was impossible. For twenty years, this man had lived in a six-by-nine-foot cell without a window. What kind of trauma would be in store for him? In tandem, I felt certain that he was too good for me. My life was full of transgressions, I just hadn't gotten caught.

"Let me know when you are out," I said, in parting. "We should have coffee."

The Merkin

My friend, Kim Merkin, was art in motion. Generous and bright, in control and rambunctious, her sumptuous home was full of naked statues and wall pieces in various poses of dance. A reminder that not only breasts, but long-hanging penises are of great importance, and good company over potluck. She organized a huge group of women that did things together. "The book club without the book," she'd explained. "You should join us."

Over time, I had with Kim and her rotating group of close to three hundred women, delighted in every thinkable fancy. We learned to sing in a round, sailed the bay on a yacht, attended countless stage performances, dressed for high tea, had an eat-Kugel-while-Kegeling party, learned hula-hoop, belly dancing, and burlesque, played polo on hobby horses, and, to celebrate fifteen years of such merriment, had a full-on *quinceañera* party, with each of us floating across the floor in ridiculous wedding-cake dresses.

Hang with valuable women, *The Artist's Way* advises. Well, if a *carpe diem* lifestyle is valuable, Kim would be Fort Knox.

Kim owned two dogs that I'd often cared for, as I'd missed my own dog so badly. Coco, a perpetually young labradoodle, required an inordinate amount of off-leash activity with other insatiable canines. The other, Alphie, was an insecure Tibetan terrier that rushed violently at other dogs. Finding a place to exercise the two together was a challenge. I decided to wrangle my daughter, Alice, into helping.

> Would you like to walk Point Isabel with me today? We can have lunch.

Point Isabel is a colossal off-leash dog park on the edge of the Bay, complete with a beach and café, a nice experience to share.

"Who owns this circus of hounds, Mama?" Alice asked, chucking the ball a full thirty yards for the inexhaustible Coco, while I kept Alphie on leash as he snarled and lunged at passing dogs.

"My friend, Kim Merkin. She runs that fun women's group I'm in."

Alice abruptly stopped walking, the wind whipping her long blonde hair in the sunlight, and folded her arms. I recognize my youth in this dusty mirror, her long slender neck, comedic facial expressions, and easy body. She flashed me her utter-shock face, reserved for a herd of charging wild boars or learning to drive stick shift in San Francisco.

"Her name is Merkin? Oh, man, that's funny. Is she a Burner?"

A Burner, should the reader be unprivy, is a brave soul that frequents the annual Burning Man festival. Upward of seventy-thousand people endure deathly hot and windy temperatures on an oceanless playa for days awaiting the burning of a colossally constructed combustible man. A shitshow of art and sex, it is not a scene for those that like to travel in comfort.

"Yes, she goes every year."

"Does she wear a *merkin*? I've got to meet this woman."

Alice's principals are modern. I've taught her everything I know about life and its foibles, cooking, gardening, and how to be civil. The rest she has learned on her own, and frequently needs to patiently bring me up to speed on.

"What's a merkin?" I asked.

"A merkin, Mama, is a vaginal wig."

My dating adventures and the bizarre hairy-vaj profile was no secret to Alice, now twenty-five. She often asked for more stories. It was she who had advised me never to go easy on graphic sex on her account.

Looking up images and information on her phone, she read the hairy history of the adornment.

An artificial covering of hair for the pubic area.

"But why?" I asked, reeling Alphie in like a kite, as he dove at a bewildered Yorkie.

Alice scanned Google to find me an answer. "Listen to this," she said. "In the fifteenth century, sex workers were ordered to shave their naughty bits to prevent the spread of public lice." She rolled her eyes, then continued. "It goes on to say that this left the women clean-shaven, much like how we imagine all women are today."

"Huh?" I blinked.

"Wait, Mom," she said. Suppressing a laugh, she continued her read. "This says women didn't shave their armpits until the early 1900s and the fad of shaving legs came along when hemlines started creeping up. And . . . shaving the pubic region is due primarily to contemporary porn and the need to *show all*." She paused for another chuckle, and then finished the article. "Anyway, the merkin was invented way back when to cover the bare skin, handy because it could also be washed and deloused! The merkin has enjoyed a resurgence for strippers and festival-goers, such as Burning Man."

"Interesting," I raised my head and gazed long over the water. On such a beautiful day, you could see San Francisco looming across the bay as clear as if it were across the street. I thought of the men I had been married to and dated; none of them ever mentioned that my vagina, well, in truth, my labia, was a problem *au naturel*. I would sometimes trim the sides for a swimsuit, but I'm not a porn star, and didn't think looking like a nine-year-old would be appealing, or comfortable.

I repeated what Alice had read. "Naughty bits? We all like to imagine women being hair-free as they are today." Taking my daughter's arm in mine, chaperone-style, I regained our stride.

"Baby?" I asked, "do you shave your bits?"

"Mother, that's not an appropriate question, but yes, I do."

How had I completely missed this? What universe was I living in? I had never reached out to the artistic nut with the "HairyVajPlease" profile, but again, I wondered what he'd say if I could ask for an explanation.

Perhaps he was trying to say, "keep it real, ladies." And why was it okay to call our most sacred region naughty?

Our arms pretzeled each other's as we proceeded slowly through the warm, salty air. Two tall frames bumping against each other affectionately. We were floating symbiosis as Alice entwined her fingers in mine. I really didn't need to learn any more, right then. I needed to think.

There is nothing comparable to a daughter, I thought, for the one millionth time. My own mother had told me that I would not understand the depth of her love for me until I myself had a daughter. Mom would have adored my once-downy-haired child, now bright-and-breezy woman, had she only been granted the gift of life beyond the age of forty-nine.

This palpable understanding kept me in the ever-present fear of leaving my daughter too soon, making every moment with her a paragon, and every subject, taste, and sensation that we shared, priceless.

Alice knew this.

We walked in silence until reaching a soft knoll and sat to eat the BLTs and artichoke I had packed. As we shared light conversation about our work, friends, and events, I unfolded slowly the story about Craig in his gated community and what I had learned there.

"I often consider how many privileged young white men from 'gated communities' of their own have made even worse choices than he did," my daughter mused. "Most of them I've known have never faced similar consequences because of their skin color. I wonder where Craig would be today if he had been born white or from the same zip code as you."

Her eyes determinedly fixed on a faraway thought. Twisting her pursed lips to the side, as if to inspect something inside of her cheek, I noticed the gesture as one she'd inherited from me. My daughter was a ferocious advocate for social justice. Her choices for every purchase were well-researched. The shoes on her feet undoubtedly secured a bicycle for a pregnant woman in Uganda.

"There is still so much work to do, Mama."

Together we found a website on my phone and ordered a gift for Kim: a red baseball cap with the words "Make a Merkin Great Again" embroidered on it. When a chilly breeze ushered in the imminent evening, we parted with a long embrace.

Protecting a daughter from being objectified is an ongoing project. The media portrays so much crap, it's exhausting. I feel as if I'd done an okay job of downplaying the overrated "hot chick machine," by continually highlighting my daughter's vast strengths. This had been no catwalk, because she did literally look like the demonized Barbie doll. Telling her that Barbie was not real didn't work on her, as she can practically fit in the doll's clothing. In her teens, she did a hilarious imitation of Tour Guide Barbie, spinning her lengthy, high-perched ponytail in a circle above her head. It was uncanny.

Alice loved dress-up and crafts, and would spend days on a project of hot glue-gunning a thousand gemstones onto a bodice and scanty panties for a rave show. Though I'd worried about her being drawn into a life ruled by her stunning physical appearance, the girl I adored was often up to her elbows in bread dough or macrame, wearing a men's flannel shirt, fighting for some feminine or racial cause.

"She is beautiful on the inside." I frequently corrected admirers. "She is an intelligent problem-solver. Her mind is remarkable. She is a leader."

"Why," the question ate at me, "would my daughter succumb to a hairless labia? Did she feel pressure from the media? Was this a trend?"

Most likely the answer was, "You don't know shit, Mama."

As I circled around the parking lot, I watched my daughter unlacing her hiking boots in the open door of her red Prius, her long, blonde hair cascading onto her knee. My vigilant love for her reminded me of the need to allow her an aircraft hangar of space. I rolled down my window.

"Just so you know," I broadcasted, as she lifted her face with a smile. "There is nothing naughty about your bits."

"I love you, Mama."

Signaling onto the crowded onramp toward my sublet bungalow, I made a vow to do more research on the subject.

The Light Within

Summertime felt right to do another photo installment of the Goddess Project. Since I was paying for the project myself, we had to wait for the spirit of the Goddess to put income under my belt, which she had, via a big corporate gig. By networking and making myself visible in the company of strong feminists, I'd found some spellbinding women of change. This would be the fourth group of women.

In late spring, I'd been asked if I could set up my studio in an art gallery run by one of my Goddesses and had shot my third group there.

During that prior session, my stylist, Emily, my camera, and I had enjoyed a brilliant array of talent. A Latina playwright, who'd created a stunning stage piece on undocumented workers, said she'd like to be dressed as a suffragette Goddess, with her power object being an antique typewriter.

Danielle, a recording artist, was a warrior with her adopted child of color. Her bow and arrow represented her success in targeting racism. Giovana, responsible for the uptown arts movement of Oakland, wore a giant, bejeweled crown. I gave her antique roller skates as her prop, since at age seventy-eight, she was impossible to keep up with.

Sarah, who ran a nonprofit specializing in climate change and green investing, donned a laurel wreath on her head, balancing an antique globe and thesaurus on her knee. And Renia, who'd introduced me to the Rotary club and their work, travelled far to build schools in poverty-stricken boroughs. She glowed in her brocade bodice and diamond headpiece dripping down her shimmering, ebony cheekbones.

Sanctifying these she-creatures was an awe-inspiring honor, as if something were being set right. My online community of neighbors seemed to have everything I needed. As if by magic, strangers just happened to have in their attics a Smith Corona typewriter, antique globe, telescope, lantern, pan flute, rabbit skin, spinning wheel—whatever I could imagine, I could acquire by simply asking.

The wardrobe closet of San Francisco's American Conservatory Theatre opened up their gargantuan cave of fantasmic garb for me to pluck through. When a Goddess Project session was scheduled, I'd return from the city, my car bursting with gowns, weapons, leathery bodices, and headpieces.

We had secured Teja of Bay Keepers, a nonprofit that legally protects our bay against polluters, and Janie, who had formed the group Women Get It Done. Lastly, we had divine, slender Ariel, who I had visions of making a badass, leather-clad angel. At age twenty-six, she was to lose her battle with cancer. Time here was of the essence.

Emily was particularly excited about this fourth session, as she had begged me to include the executive director of Gender Forward, Jessica, who was in the process of transitioning and had been a guiding force for Emily's son, who was identifying as a girl. Though only eight years old, Emily's child had no doubt in her mind who she was, and putting the light on gender was important to Em. I'd agreed it was a wonderful idea and put her on the task of talking with Jessica about her vision and finding a suitable date for her flight up from Los Angeles.

Together, Emily and I planned the style.

"Ariel is hair-challenged from the cancer, but we can do a glorious upknot in an exotic scarf—she has plenty—or enjoy her baldness. My vision is a strong leather corset over a wildly living floral skirt. I have a huge set of wings for her. Oh, and that shoulder-to-shoulder brass falcon medallion. Let's put a bird on her, for sure."

"Put a bird on it." Emily smiled, as she scrawled notes as fast as I could talk.

"For Teja, I found an antique telescope she can hold and a nautical map she can stand on. I'll get her a pirate hat and dress at American Conservatory Theater. I found a killer headpiece for Janie. I'm going to buy her some boxing gloves."

I liked to buy my Goddess' power pieces and give them as a gift. A kind of trophy for them to keep, along with a large-framed print.

"Have you spoken with our Gender Forward executive, Jessica?" I asked.

"Yes, *he's* flying up Friday." Emily paused with one of her I-have-news-for-you looks. "And, guess what?"

I waited.

"Jessica is now Jack."

"I love it! I'm so happy for her. Talk about a strong woman. Wow, I really can't wait to meet her now."

"*Him*, Reen. You're going to need some social guidance before *he* gets here. You can't just bumble through this. The challenge will be dressing him as a Goddess."

It meant a lot to me that Emily was on this journey with me. She knew so much about the delicacy and intensity of the LGBTQ culture. Learning about it was important to both of us.

I reached out to Jack to work out the perfect outfit for his session, and let the other girls know what the situation was. Not one batted an eye, because they were, after all, Goddesses.

The following week, we assembled in the studio. I'd let Scoundrel know that we were going to be using the space for the entire day. He was fine with that. He had planned a day at the beach with the broker.

Emily began by busying herself on Ariel's makeup, complimenting her on her flawless skin. Her mother, Naomi, had come to watch.

Of course, her skin was flawless, we congruently thought. She's twenty-six.

I had photographed Naomi and Ariel for a mother-daughter portrait when this little Goddess was fourteen years old. She was dazzling on the brink of womanhood, with raven hair gleaming down her slender back.

Her mesmerizing green eyes revealed her to be professedly closer to God than most. Sometimes you can sense those with short lives. Bright stars burn so fast, whereas assholes seem to never die.

My eyes swiveled up to meet Naomi's. She was at the finish line of letting go of a daughter the same age as my own. I'm sure she had cried as many tears as there had been hair on this angel's head, probably more. Putting Naomi's heart into mine, I hoped she could feel my spell of empathy.

"Okay, she's ready," chirped Emily. "I made her lips super red. Is that okay?"

As I tested the lights, Emily wriggled Ariel into her gigantic wings.

"You put Victoria Secret models to shame," she said, as she smiled and backed up to check Ariel's clothes.

"Oh, the pup!" Emily remembered. Ariel's little dog had been so quiet, resting in the corner, that we'd forgotten he was her chosen power object. A little white Bichon Frise, completely oblivious to his importance, probably because he couldn't understand what was to happen to his human companion.

I turned on two turbo fans to levitate her wings, and set the music. Music is always essential in setting the mood for a subject.

Just then a celestial song came through my often intuitive sound system. As though calling to angels, our hearts joined with an unspoken prayer of guidance, wondering, which way do we go? How do we get through the unfair catastrophe of a young, brilliant light burning out?

While we were shooting, Jack and the other Goddesses streamed in silently. Seeing that we were working, they took a seat next to Emily who made them feel welcome with big hugs. Together, they watched silently.

To be completely frank, I don't know very much about photography. My camera has scores of bells and whistles I never use. When gear-freaks interrogate me on my technique, I usually deflect them by saying, "I take the lens cap off." I suppose if you do anything long enough you can hone in on perfection, or whatever meaning lies in waiting. I believe it is my yearning for story and great respect for the light that comes through.

When I finished, I set my camera on the counter with a sigh, eyes wet, then folded myself in an embrace with Naomi, where we stayed for a full minute, our bodies convulsing in a weeping fit. The room was still and spinning at the same time. Electricity filled the air.

"Wow, what a trip," said Jack. "I'm so thrilled to be here."

This would be my first time meeting Jack—a moment I had so looked forward to. I know lots of men and I know lots of women. This one was changing from one to the other. What was my role here?

"And I am so thrilled too, Jack." I instinctively gave him a hug, reacting to the sensation of the room. It was a wondrous experience to feel his strong shoulders. I knew instantly that this was a man and I wanted him to feel welcome, accepted, and celebrated.

I showed Jack the clothing we had pulled from the wardrobe for him and asked if I could dress him.

"Here, see if these pants fit," I said, offering up some loose fitting white trousers.

"I'd rather keep my black pants on if that's okay."

"Absolutely, you'll know when we get there. What do you think of this?" I asked, offering up a white collarless Shakespearean blouse pleated at the shoulders.

"Love it," he said, as he slipped off his T-shirt, examining the blouse for its flouncy opening. As his T came off, I noticed his chest. Obviously, post-double-mastectomy, it was tattooed with a manuscript of words in many colors and fonts.

"Whoa, wait," I said, holding his shirt. "This looks important."

"It is my story." He looked at me, both defiant and proud, puffing his chest like a teenaged lad.

It was difficult to make out the words, but he was able to explain to me that it was after his bout with cancer and the loss of both breasts that he recognized himself in this strong barrel chest.

"What a brave man you are," I said, as I wrapped a seventeenth century Brummell cravat around his neck, giving him the air of a French mercenary.

Our eyes met to exchange approval and I checked my senses. I felt both the warmth of a woman and the testosterone of a man.

"I found your power object," I said, pulling out of a black bag an old beat-up lantern from the Second World War.

"Perfect," he said.

When asked the prior week what physical object Jack would consider that might illustrate his power, he had challenged me with a lantern. "An old one that has been through a lot. Beat up, bent, and chinked, but still working. One with a strong light, like a beacon."

I'd worried about how this was going to go. How the narrative might change having a guy as a Goddess in my book. What he would wear and how he would feel. How mixing these particular people together in a room, all in different phases of this life, would work out.

I had opted to let go and "let her" decide what it was supposed to look like. A collection of women celebrating exactly what and where they were on this bumpy ride. One middle-aged, feeling sturdy, one young, striving toward a path of service, one valiantly surrendering to the abyss of death, and one trusting that she was meant to be him.

All of these brethren and *sistren*, following the brilliant circles of light to love. Each on a dissimilar path and all worthy and fortified by our collective support.

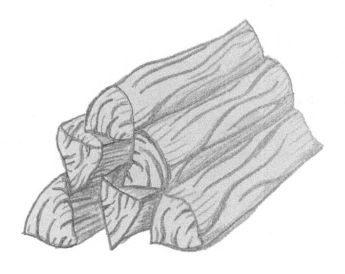

Errand Boy

I'd been seeing Paul for a few weeks. I met him at a Greg Kihn concert. Need I say more.

I had gone with an old friend, Betsy, always game to go to pretty much any kind of music. She shared with me an eclectic ear to the passing greats like the Counting Crows and the Eurythmics. Prior to the show, we were dining at Jupiter, a pizza joint, when a cute, outspoken kid walked by and made a comment about how foxy we were.

"What a creep," Betsy spit, although I found his advances adorable.

An hour later at the show, he just had to tell us what a coincidence it was that we were both there.

"Do you like short Jewish boys?" he clumsily blurted.

I had to think about it. "I guess it depends on the qualities of the short Jewish boy."

Scoundrel was at the show (naturally) and we all stormed the stage to "Jeopardy." Perhaps it was Scoundrel's presence that allowed me to accept Paul's kiss after the show. We exchanged numbers.

Paul was clearly too young. I knew nothing would come from this, but his persistence was like a comedic hobby. I wasn't seeing anyone else at the time, and he was easy, as was I.

Paul was a fourth-grade schoolteacher a few towns away, working on a book of sports poetry, whatever that is. He loved to talk about his cock, which he purposely misspelled in his frequent texts, as if in code, his lewdness would come across with less offense.

> Would you like a piece of my Jewish c&ck?

> My Jewish c&ck wants your wet pussy.

> How bout some humping with my Jewish c&ck?

> Ready to moan with my Jewish c&ck at your place on Hampel Street?

I thought of my Jewish friends and clients. All of them were gentle, intelligent, engaging, and purposeful. Had he not been Mitzvahed?

"Could you keep religion out of this?" I asked him one evening. "It leaves a bad taste in my mouth. You are the furthest thing from Jewish in my mind."

Most of the time, I ignored him and just threw my head back to laugh at his ridiculous timing, centered around recess and after-school care. Once in a broad while, I would invite him over for some completely unsatisfying encounter where he would beg for compliments. He was a child, and I was leading him on, basically for fodder of this investigation of what makes men do what they do.

It finally became excruciating, when, while presenting a PowerPoint lecture on the history of Lake Merritt to a crowded downtown ballroom, his text dinged up on the upper right of the projected screen.

> School's out. Let's hump on
> Hampel!

I thought I would die. Fortunately, the message seemed to have gone unnoticed by the majority of the crowd. Only one close friend blew water out of her nose.

What had I become? I didn't need this guy, I hardly even liked him. I decided it was time to sit him down, face-to-face, and let him know this was going nowhere.

> Why don't you come
> over this evening and we
> can talk.

Dani, out of town on her own fool's errand, was happy this affair was coming to an end.

> Thank God. What a
> loser. I've been patiently
> awaiting that nightmare
> to end. Good luck, Reen.

Later that evening, our relationship burned itself out almost as fast as the firewood Mike had given me the last time I saw him.

> I'm just leaving my place,
> headed your way.

> Can you pick up some
> firewood on your way?
> I'm just about out.

> I don't want to. I've been
> around enough people
> today. I'm not your
> errand boy.

> I thought that was precisely what you were. Why don't you just stay home, and please stop texting me. This is over.

As I put the last log on the fire, I picked up my flute to practice "Go Tell Aunt Rhody," when my phone actually rang, not a beep signaling a text, but an actual ring.

Thurston

Thurston Chaterly IV said, "We talked several months ago, but never met."

I set my flute down to think back. I was painfully aware of how many men I had texted, spoken to, and made plans with. The sheer number was unreckonable. This was no longer a search for the right guy; it had turned into a circus. Paul had been an absolute joke. Prior to him, worth only brief mention, had been a Guatemalan kid who sang beautiful love ballads in Spanish. Then there was Maurice, visiting from Paris for work, who came over for dinner one evening in his charming scarf. He was so French and made a one-night stand feel so natural. I was experimenting with freedom, forgetting that what I was really searching for was a practical partner.

"Oh, yes, Thurston, I remember." It was months ago and I'd been driving, which I do poorly, so had been unable to give him my full attention. I do recall that he sounded like an interesting fellow. His name alone beckoned the historian in me.

"I was hoping to patch things up with my ex, but it has become increasingly clear that it will never work. I keep thinking about you and wonder if perhaps we could meet?"

"Are you close by? Do you have any firewood?" I asked.

This was supposed to be a private joke between me and myself, reminding me how bizarre my behavior had become.

"I do," he said.

I looked at my phone: 7:10.

"It's a lovely evening. Come over. I've got cheese."

I went out on the patio for a last cigarette before brushing my teeth and smoothing my hair. I heard a text come in from Thurston.

> I can't have sex with you if we are not in a relationship.

What a peculiar thing to say. Was that supposed to be an advance or a tease?

Fifteen minutes later, I opened the door to a lovely, tall man about my age. Silver hair topped his fine, strong jaw, and, as I had hoped, he had the look of an old-world British family. He had a prefab fire log and a bottle of wine in his arms. I opted not to explain about the log request, but rather, thanked him and set it on the dying fire. It lit up immediately, as if starting a new chapter.

We sat by the fire and talked for hours. He was a business owner for an analytics company that had an office here and another in Europe, where he spent half of his time. He was interested in my work, and loved the art Dani and I had compiled in our little bungalow.

"What are you looking for?" he asked, as if this were a job interview.

"Thank you for asking," I set my hand on his knee and folded my legs up on the sofa. "I'd been beginning to think that I'd forgotten. Honestly, I want to go home. I have a great house waiting for me. I want a partner I can care for and be cared for by. I was built for family. When I find my man, I'll be knitting him a sweater with little deer on it. I'll be organizing the books and cooking dinner. There, I said it."

"But your work is good. Don't you need time for that?"

"I can do both."

From my experience, men had been attracted to the independence I'd been exhibiting, and I'd have to say, I was enjoying watching myself try it on. I had plenty of friends in mediocre marriages, which I knew was behind me, yet I longed for a partner. I needed to be taken care of. Thurston was easy to talk to. I had things to sort out, as did he. I decided that he would be a good friend, if nothing else.

As he left, his kiss assured me that it could be something else. I drifted off to sleep thinking this feeling reminded me of Morgan, but this one was real.

The following morning Thurston texted a single word.

> WOW

I jumped from bed and did a happy dance, restraining myself from answering too soon.

Opening my laptop, I started doing some research on him. Indeed the fourth, his great grandfather had worked on the incandescent bulb with Edison. He was a prosperous business owner who had recently taken over another analytics company and was moving fast, most of the time in Paris. Yet beyond that, he was a dreamboat who made my body ache. He embodied what I was attracted to: solid. Are there really any solid men left? I wondered.

A few hours later, he texted.

> I need a lamp.

> Uhuru Furniture on Grand Avenue. The owner is a genius with consignment. Everything is beautiful, useful and memorable. I'm at the hardware store across the street.

I rushed to my car to get there before he could discover my lie.

Did you find one? I can cross the street and help if you'd like.

Yes, come.

I parked in the hardware store parking lot and crossed the street. It was a balmy afternoon, so I had put on cutoff jeans.

Thurston was hard to miss, substantially larger than anyone else in the crowded antique store. Wearing a smug expression, he was holding two lamps. One, with a colorful glaze, had ceramic birds at the base, the other, black and contemporary. Beside him trailed a little girl.

"Hi Reenie," he smiled. "This is Amber, my daughter." He pointed with his elbow down at his little mascot, his hands full.

This was his six-year-old. He had, the previous night, shown me pictures of this daughter. I was charmed that he allowed me to meet her so soon and wondered if he had prepared her for this or if happenstance was his plan.

"I like the birds," Amber lisped. "It matches the birds on my pillows."

"Well, then, it's settled."

After paying for his treasure, Amber skipped happily down the street in front of Thurston and me.

"We were about to get some lunch. Would you care to join us?"

I couldn't believe my luck. Could this be happening? Just out of the blue comes this dreamboat with a daughter and he's allowing me into their universe so quickly? The answer was *yes*.

We found a casual spot with outdoor tables littered with board games. We selected one where we all wore crowns with a card facing out and needed to guess, twenty-questions-wise, what we were.

I was an airplane, literally. Watching this man-parent with his adorable crown was extremely attractive. It seemed as if metal objects surrounding us were sliding across the floor toward our magnetism. His furtive smile made me long to touch him, but I didn't.

"Hey Thurston, we are having a dinner party this Sunday. We call it Salubrious Sunday Symposium, where we have twelve guests for an alfresco event. Everyone has to bring a song or poem and a bottle of wine.

Would you care to join us?" Dani would be proud that I had landed someone worthy as a dinner partner.

"Thank you so much for the invite, but I'm afraid I leave for Paris tomorrow for work. I will be gone for ten days, but if you are around tonight?"

I cancelled my plans to go to the roller derby with Kim Merkin's ladies' group and bought a nice salmon to grill. Dani would not return until the morning, thus I laundered the sheets in the hopes I might have an overnight guest.

Thurston Chaterly IV arrived on time in khaki shorts, a bottle of Chardonnay, and a long and deep kiss. I was wearing my short navy jersey dress, cut low, with my cowboy boots.

After a superb meal on the back patio, under the Keebler Elf walnut tree, I brought out some lemon ice cream.

"*Mmm*, you make?" he exclaimed with his mouth full.

"Always."

He reached over and gave me a lemony kiss, licking the tangy cream that rested on my lips.

"I wish I could stay." His eyes were apologetic.

"Then you may. You're all grown up. I won't keep you up late."

"I'm in some pretty intense therapy for a condition I have. I'm a sex addict."

I pulled back to sit squarely in front of him. Oh man, what now? Another fallout from a traumatic childhood, a funky mother, or unscrupulous lover? What am I, a social worker? This was another situation where I am supposed to play either therapist or hard to get. Yet I really didn't have the mindset to do either. He was there and I wanted a piece of him.

"You're not allowed to have sex?" I tried to understand.

"Not unless I am in a relationship."

"Well, I can relate to that," I purred, giving him another kiss.

It was especially easy to get Thurston between the sheets. Once he surrendered, he was consumed. Was I being selfish or hoping that I could advance us into a relationship to make this act legal? Definitely the latter. I genuinely liked this guy. We were an absolute fit. I was certain I could bring him to Jesus, or in this case, the Goddess.

He left before morning, not with the rapturous joy I was experiencing, but with complete remorse. We had conversed a lot over the last two evenings, and I felt convinced he was beyond his previous relationship. Yet his behavior implied that he had been untrue to someone. Ten days in Paris, I resolved, would be good for the both of us.

When I awoke, I longed to look at him one more time before he left and texted.

> I have a book for you to read on the plane. May I drop it before you leave?

He gave me his address, and, on my way to pick up some pies for the afternoon's Salubrious Symposium, buzzed him in his high-rise apartment in downtown Oakland. The elevator opened on the top floor to the penthouse. The glassy view was expansive. There, in the living room, a tuba and a cello, balanced on stands.

"My car is on the way," he said, running, buttoning his shirt, his tie dangling. I was struck again with the how-did-you-get-so-lucky sting.

I handed him the book, *Your Six-Year-Old: Loving and Defiant.*

"Are you in some kind of trouble?" I searched his eyes.

"No, no. It just happened so fast."

We kissed—a good one. When we hugged, my head resting on his broad shoulder, he pulled away first.

"Lean out, girl," I whispered on the elevator ride down. "Lean out."

The following days were dizzy and dazzling. I loved working out with my Pilates class, swam three times a week, and had two joyful newborn photo sessions. I avoided reaching out to Thurston. He was real, not a catfisher, and that was all that mattered for now.

At the end of a glistening Tuesday, I went up to the club to take a hot tub. This had been part of the Scoundrel's routine, and I knew, it being five o'clock, I risked running into him and his vodka cranberry. Lowering myself slowly into the deliciously clean and hot water, I chatted with an acquaintance named Joe. His name was easy to remember because I could recall his nickname given by Mike had been "Smart Joe."

"How's Mike?" he asked, fanning his hands through the hot water. Joe was one of the few people at the club who knew that Mike and I had split up. We kept it under wraps, since Mike was kind enough to allow the membership to continue to be ours.

"Who knows? I think he's well."

"I can hear him when he drives through town blaring Tom Petty out of his car," he chuckled.

"Yup, that would be him. *Ope!* Speak of the devil!"

I'd know the walk from a mile away. Sauntering toward us with an obviously concealed beverage under his towel. He always walked fast, like he was two steps in front of the constable.

"Hi, Smart Joe!" chirped Mike, slipping in the hot water with his usual loud exhale and "*oooh yeeeah*" expression. Turning to me, he glanced quickly to see which swimsuit I was wearing and smiled approvingly. The only one-piece he ever bought me, because it was cut so low.

"You should have told me you were coming. I would have brought you a drink. Here, I'll share." He extended his drink with his always surprising, impatient urgency. I took a pull on his familiar plastic cocktail glass and suddenly it was a year ago without a care in the world. That fruit punch flavor represented everything carefree.

"Yum, thank you," I said, smiling.

Joe watched dumbfoundedly as we chatted about dogs and photo sessions and mutual friends. It was strange to everyone that we continued to be civil as if the annihilation of our empire had never happened. I should have been furious. I just wasn't. He should have taken away this club membership, our shared studio, my leased car. He just didn't. We danced around it because it was the easiest thing to do.

"How's the Mortgage Broker?" I asked.

"She's great. We're buying a vacation rental in Sonoma County."

I winced. "Fuck you, Scoundrel."

I had begged him for an investment property when we were together. She had some kind of magical power over him that I never had.

He loved to hear me cuss, almost as much as my stories. "Who are you dating, now?"

"I met a guy. He's in Paris for a few weeks. When he gets back, I'll see where we are."

"Another catfish? Come on! You have to meet them first, Puka."

Pukalani was the title Mike had given me in Hawaii, where we vacationed every spring. It's the name of a glorious waterfall where people like to have weddings. To hear him call me this again, astride hearing of the great fortune he was having with this new girl, was a test. I searched my heart for strength, and for five long beats, I wanted to cry. I wanted back in.

"You're not going back. You're going forward," assured the Goddess. "You've already been there. There is a divine plan for you."

"It means a great deal to me that you look out for me," was all I could muster.

Taking in a deep breath, I submerged myself so I could be alone under the hot, bubbling water. I felt grateful for this enveloping heat and the relief it offered. Pulling my tongue back in my throat, I thought of Mother. I felt her warm hand on my forehead as I lost myself in her suspension. I didn't want to come up, but I had to. When I did, Mike was gone. Smart Joe was still there, resting his lips against his fist, he looked at me for a full minute.

"You've got this, girl."

I wondered if Joe was single.

That evening, I finally heard from Thurston. He called at 11:00 p.m., which would have been 8:00 a.m. in Paris. I liked that he was primarily a phoner rather than a texter.

"I'm just going to sleep," I told him. "How has the trip been going?"

He described his work, his office there, the restaurants, and the street-lights. It was far too early in our relationship to say something stupid like, "Take me next time! Get me the fuck out of here." So, rather, I said, "I hope to see Paris again soon. Last time, I went with my daughter. It was divine."

"What are you wearing?" he purred.

"I'm in bed. Flossed, polished, moisturized, and naked as a jaybird."

"Are you wearing panties?"

"Oh my," I thought, "where is this going?"

"Would you like to have phone sex?" he asked, taking a low, deep breath in.

I thought of my catfisher, Morgan, again.

"I suppose this is popular for those who travel a lot," I said. "I can give it a go."

Thurston gave me suggestions of where and when to put my hand, while he murmured his desires to me. Honestly, I felt a bit silly.

"You are very sweet, Thurston, and I don't want to ruin your fun. But I think I might rather wait until you come home and see you in person."

I texted Thurston a few times over the next few weeks and received no acknowledgement. The confusion was palpable.

"Maybe he died," Dani rationalized. "Is his dating profile still up?"

"It's not," I said. "I imagine he went back to his ex."

I heard from Thurston a year later. He had seen me on Facebook asking for donations of analog cameras for a darkroom class I was teaching to high school students. He asked if I would meet him for a drink.

"What happened to you?" I asked. "You ghosted me."

"I was afraid that I wanted to touch you."

Thurston looked wan. He was thinner than he had been in the past, and I was taken with how much older he looked. I remembered that he was two years my senior. This would mean, nearing sixty, he was still struggling with an addiction that probably wouldn't plague him much longer. But what did I know?

I had really wanted this guy. If I'd been able to secure a life with him, it would have been hell dancing around this complication. My healthy reverence of intimacy would have been squandered. I thought to ask if he'd found a new romance or patched up an old one. I thought of asking about his daughter, who would have been near eight by now. I resolved to let it slide. The Goddess had clearly allowed me to dodge that bullet.

"Here," he grinned and handed me a well-worn camera with a calcified wraparound case and strap. It was heavy, indicating a metal body. I adeptly unsnapped the case and swiveled it open.

A 1970 Minolta X-300. I'd know it like my own hand. It was the precise model that Dad had given me for my first single-lens camera when I was a teenager. The musty aroma of an attic was intoxicating.

I lifted it to my eye to check the stop and speed. So many of the cameras donated for this project were toast. Snapping a shot of Thurston, I cocked the trigger and felt a pull.

"Oh, there's a roll in here." I said, instinctively depressing a tiny button on the undercarriage to wind the film back into its canister. Pulling the back open, I tipped the roll into my palm and offered it up to Thurston.

"You can throw that away," he said.

"No, never. It's Kodachrome. This is gold. Your memories lie in this can."

Thurston didn't feel the same value that I did, so I sent it out to process. There were only seven slides on the roll. Several images of a very young Thurston with a girl on a beach, his hand resting comfortably on her hip. Her halter top and feathered hair indicated that it was probably around 1980. He would have been in graduate school. Had this been the girl that had scarred Thurston? Was his desire for her somehow shamed or derailed, causing his irreparable damage?

The last image was of an older man sitting at the bar in the restaurant where I had seen him last. I examined the slides long and hard.

"What a shame," I whispered, feeling deep love over an exquisitely formed and talented person. Men are so fragile.

In July, Walter Shaub, the Director of the US Office of Government Ethics, resigned. President Trump held a bilateral meeting with Mexican President Enrique Pena Nieto to reiterate that Mexico was to pay for the border wall. Several meetings were held to repeal and replace the Affordable Care Act. Anthony Scaramucci (the Mooch) was appointed as Trump's new White House Communications Director, only to be fired ten days later. Trump stated that transgender individuals would not be accepted in any capacity in the US military, and during a speech addressing law enforcement officers at Suffolk County Community College, he called for increased border security. Referencing (or joking) about the possible use of police brutality, he received applause from the crowd.

Christian

When I hear the ominous hoot of an owl in the night, well, that's Mom. She's letting me know that I need to be still and listen. She does this spasmodically, regardless of where I am living. "Hey!" she screeches, "listen, child. You are at a fork in the road and we need to talk about this." So we do, and the collective decision is always the right one for me. Big decisions like kids' schools, travel, and life steps can be intimidating alone. She comes in gently, as mothers often do, making the navigation appear to be my own. It is striking that the owl can find me wherever I happen to be living.

Similarly, when I hear the auditory bombardment of a passing motorcycle, with its uneven firing of a V-twin, well, that is Christian. The sensation is as profound as my mother's visits. The throaty, erratic snarl sets up a visceral sensation that can only be calmed with a rehearsed ritual. Deep breath, then I am preconditioned to say aloud, "Hi, Christian."

Each time, my brain recalls exactly the sound of his breathy voice, "Hey there. It's me."

There were many occasions when I would pull over and stare into space for two or three minutes, leaning in hard to the starving bruise, finding small consolation that pain is similar to pleasure in its depth.

It was never going to work with him.

Sometimes I run through old voice messages on my phone, all beginning with, "Hey there, it's me," to gauge the distance between my heart and that loss.

He'd listed himself on OkCupid for a week, if that. I, with my vast experience of online dating, recognized him immediately as a rarity, and set a date with him the very evening I saw his profile.

"Thank you for initiating this," Christian said at the bar at Bellanico, a short walk up from Dani and my little Glenview bungalow. He had a soft, blonde mustache that extended to encircle his chin, stopping at his dimples. His eyes twinkled like a slender Santa Claus and immediately put me at ease. His button-up shirt was lined with a different, patterned interfacing than the one showing—paisley on the inside, stripes on the outside. One of those you don't go out and buy, but rather, a clothier comes to your house and measures you for. I found this, in combination with the fact that he'd arrived on a motorcycle, very alluring.

"I was at Pixar for a while. My team created a little film called *Geri's Game*."

"Oh, yeah." This was exciting to me, having worked in animation for a short stint in my life. "The old man who played chess with himself! I loved that piece. Gosh, I remember when the first short came out with the lamp bouncing into the scene. Computer animation was so cutting edge."

I knew from his profile that he was forty-two. He'd have been young at the time *Geri's Game* came out.

"I lived in a tiny house with three other guys all working in animation. I met Amy when I was there. That's how I ended up with this." He pulled out his phone and thumbed through photos, landing on one of him and his daughter. I knew he had a daughter from his profile questionnaire:

Do you have kids? Yes, a daughter.

Do you want more? No. But will enjoy others' kids. The same category that I had listed myself in.

His little girl, around eight years old, was perfect. Her long, blonde hair framed gentle hazel eyes and crooked bilaterals.

"She's lovely. So, Amy is your ex-wife?"

"No. We never married, but we're good friends, and she's been very supportive through my divorce from Julie."

I also knew from his profile that his breakup was fresh. I backed away from the subject so early in our accord.

"Where are you working, now?" I asked, ordering another Tempranillo in an inordinately large glass.

"Nowhere." He looked down.

I thought I saw an ember from his sparkling eyes fall onto his hand.

"I was working for a cell tower company but left it to start a career in viticulture. I don't know what's going to happen, now." His eyes were now desolate.

I thought I'd written the book on desolate, but this was different. Something was frightening him, and I longed to hold him like I would a child. It was as if he couldn't catch his breath. I wanted to pick up the tear from the back of his hand and put it back in his eye to regain its sparkle.

When he walked me home, we came in through the back gate. The Keebler Elf yard had much to offer, so I plugged in the carnival lights. The sudden illumination was like the beginning of a grand production. We sat for a while at the cloth-covered table with a huge flower arrangement of specimens I'd foraged from the neighborhood: maple, camelias, willows, and heath.

"It's really nice out here." he said, breathing in the warm, balmy air. The walk from the bar had been fragrant and enveloping, the pittosporum trees setting the stage for a sublime summer night.

"Make this last," I thought. There was so much we didn't know about each other, and I anticipated the evening as one of much sharing.

"Tell me about your ex-wife," I offered up, feeling that it might be an okay time.

Unraveling the yore of the ex-wife is a perennial activity when dating at my age. Everyone is at a different stage of being alone. Talking about the reason why is the first step to healing.

"It just happened so fast." He pushed hard on his eye to stop a tear. "I thought we were just trying a reset. But after just a few weeks she said, 'Christian, we're getting a divorce.'"

"Maybe it's too soon," I said, "Maybe she'll feel the void and you'll get back together."

"No, she's already filled the void. She will never be alone."

Just then, Dani's bedroom door, which opened onto the backyard, cracked open.

"Is that you, Reen?" She was protective of our little home, always checking on any nefarious sounds. I was relieved for the distraction.

"Yes, dear. Come on out. I'd like you to meet someone."

Dani came out in a sweatshirt and shorts. I felt proud to live with such a welcoming presence. She always approached new people like the gentle mother that she was.

Bringing out a bottle of her famous Cline collection, we sat for an additional hour, and, in tandem, explained to Christian how and why we got in this little house together. Demonstrating our ease in experimenting with our completely new life, devoid of clutter, he seemed visibly comforted. She then walked him through the house and flaunted our tacky art collection, resting on the three-bliss' volleyball photograph.

"Ridiculous." He chuckled.

"We should have Christian come to the next Salubrious, Reen."

"Absolutely." I smiled at the two of them. "I think he'd fit in nicely."

This felt like a good time to end our date, so I suggested I walk him up the block to his motorcycle. As we walked, I told him about the workings of our Sunday Salubrious Symposium.

When we reached his parking spot, I marveled at his beautiful chariot, well, more like a Transformer robot or Batmobile.

"Aprila," he called it, and when he threw his sturdy leg over the top, I nearly collapsed from desire. I had no choice but to kiss him.

I remembered his profile had disclosed that he was a ridiculously good kisser. I was able to verify this as true. Like magnet and iron, we couldn't stop. I literally heard the whir of a Vibraslap—the instrument that Cake uses on the song, "Short Skirt/Long Jacket."

Whirrrrrrrrrrrz

"I'm taking my daughter to Disneyland tomorrow. I'll be gone for four days."

"Send pictures." I kissed him. "Perhaps we can see each other when you get back?"

"I'd like that," he said, resting his forehead on mine. I breathed in just one last kiss.

"May I ask a favor?"

"Anything."

"Get me a coin purse, any Disney character will do."

He returned with a red, sparkly Mickey Mouse wallet that was just the right size for my purse named Bonnie.

The following weeks were full-on infatuation. Walking around Lake Merritt, we clutched onto each other like two koala bears, stopping every forty feet to hug and kiss, again and again. His eyes sparkled at me as I laid out picnics of fried chicken and apples. Our newfound crush danced like ribbons in my breezy, rapturous heart. He was tall, with a huge, strong body and graceful lope. When he held my hand, my whole body illuminated.

I crafted the best of everything for Christian, offering only the finest. Salubrious Sundays now included Veuve Clicquot and oysters. I brought his daughter and him swimming at Scoundrel's club, arranged meetings with the most creative folks from my circle.

I had semi-permanent eyelashes installed, and even experimented with Botox. Everything was falling into place. Yet, there was something I wasn't harkening.

The eyelash extensions had been a gift certificate from Alice, who had a full set. She'd pulled off the darling kitty look with significantly more *savoir faire* than I did. Mine didn't last the predicted two months, as I rubbed my eyes too frequently, and led a more outdoorsy lifestyle than millennial girls. Within a week, I'd find lashes in my soup, on my pillow, or in my cleavage. Yet, I'd enjoyed skipping the dreaded mascara portion of the morning routine, and thus returned for a second installment of extensions.

Lash extensions require a full hour of sitting still, a long time for such a superfluous folly. Concerned that I might get hungry during my session, I stopped at a coffee shop near the salon to pick up a muffin. Across the strip mall, I noticed a storefront with a neon hand on the front window with the words "Psychic Readings" on it.

"I'm surprised," I told my lash-lady, as I lay on my back, eyes closed, "to see a soothsayer shop in such a prime retail space. Whoever runs the place must be making some kind of profit."

"She's very good," Claudia said, as she meticulously applied my mink lashes, one after another, with her tweezers. "Her name is Tangerine. She's the real deal."

I love it.

When we were at last finished, I trotted downstairs with my heavy lids and waved my forty bucks over the tarot cards, which Tangerine promptly splayed over the entire table.

After a long, deep breath, she closed her eyes, then opened them slowly to meet mine. Next to her sat her teenage daughter, who I assumed was apprenticing to learn her mother's skills. Her cell phone continually chirping incoming texts, she appeared less than intent.

Not me, though. Truth or not, I couldn't think of a place I would rather be than in the presence of a clairvoyant priestess, be she self-appointed or ordained. The room was divinely yielding, with dark velvet drapery, richly upholstered pillows, and fragrant candles. A little slice of Romania, right there on a suburban main street.

"You have been on a long journey," she crooned, her dark eyes enveloping me.

"You are safe on your foray. By next year, you will be home. I'm excited for you."

"You have been wronged by a man named *M-M-M-Mike?*"

"Oh, my God," I thought, squirming in my chair.

Closing her eyes once more, she inhaled slowly, knotted her forehead as if she was trying to capture an elusive, disturbing vision, then, with a securing exhale, bore her eyes into me again. First, with apology, and then, with a sisterish concern, she extolled carefully, "Beware the salt-and-pepper man. There is something you don't know about him. He will destroy your work. Watch where you step."

The following day, Christian visited me in the studio and we made love on my favorite chair to gypsy music. It was epic. Then I looked, for the first time, beyond his eyes and thighs and lips and hands.

"Your hair," I noted, while I refastened my bra at the waist, turning it around to pull it into place. "Would you say it is salt-and-pepper?"

Christian made me so happy that I told him frequently, "you make me so happy." When I was with him, I was happy, when I was without him, I was miserable.

I became acutely aware of love songs, running the soundtrack of what seemed to narrate the phase. "I see your face in every flower." I became fixated on how I could see him again. I marked my calendar with the recurring event, "Christian Available," as every other week his girl would be with her mother. But these feelings were primarily mine. Though we had so many great events together, "Christian Available" didn't mean that at all.

What I was not accepting was the truth, because I didn't want to.

After a borderline platonic relationship with Amy, the mother of his daughter, Christian had opted to marry conceivably the wealthiest heiress in California. The marriage lasted just five years, and had not proven to be the most prudent decision for his child. He'd signed a prenup without reviewing it, and just a month prior to our meeting, had been thrown off that train with no explanation beyond the obvious: the princess was through with her toy.

Unemployed and completely without direction, Christian was a wreck. Finding his own way, following any circle of light, he found solace in his regained relationship with his daughter, long winding rides on his Italian motorcycle, and tearful, unraveling conversations.

Sometimes he would lead me into his apartment near the lake, a catastrophic avalanche from his painfully recent life with the heiress in her castle. He would show me his stamp collection or family photos, handling each as if it were a road map or magic key.

"Here is my dad," he would explain. "He and Mom wove baskets and sold them at the farmer's market. They are both gone now."

He'd stop, searching the air around him for the answer with welling eyes.

I borrowed a friend's cabin on the Russian River for several days to write, sing, and woo him. When he arrived at the cabin on his motorcycle, I stood on the deck, looking down at his rugged frame unbuckling his helmet and whispered to myself, "Breathe it in, sister. It doesn't get any better than this."

Building a fire in the pit on the edge of the river, I set up some chairs with a view of the ducks and occasional egret. The silence was spellbinding.

"The cool thing about a river," I started, as I opened a bottle of wine, "is that her energy is free. She just keeps running and you never need to restart her or pay for it in any way except to be honest with her."

Christian settled his gaze on the shimmering water, the prisms changing from white to mossy green and back again as the river rollicked the surface, offering diamonds. He searched the mesmerizing glitter.

"You can tell her everything," I whispered. "When I return to the river, I try to find a special rock to sit on and wait. She always starts with,

'Hi . . . or in your case . . . hey there, how have you been?' You can spend hours with a river."

Standing up, as if by demand, Christian set his wine glass on the ground and teetered down, his hands out sideways as he balanced down the treacherous, rocky path to the water's edge. Something advised me not to follow, but rather, watch from a distance. He carefully selected his granite perch and sat. No more than forty feet away, he seemed small next to the river, which was a new vantage for me. I moved up into the cabin to find something to eat, and forty minutes later, looking off the deck, he was still in counsel on his chosen boulder.

When our vacation ended, I felt like our crush had descended into something else. I wasn't sure what it was, but the luster had desaturated.

"Christian is not going to take care of you, Mom." my son Henry explained to me a few days later, as, high on a ladder, he readjusted the carnival lights in Jim's yard. "He's flaky."

Flaky?

This had never occurred to me.

"He's very handsome, but as you have told me thousands of times, it's not the most important thing."

I had told Henry that countless times. Henry, like his father, was very handsome, and frequently I would tease him with the comment to put him in his place.

Not interested in hearing what wisdom my son had to share, I went on to fantasize about my life with Christian and his daughter. They would move into my Snake Road home with me. I would get a dog or a set of kittens. Christian would receive a gigantic settlement from his ex-wife and his daughter would swing happily in the hammock with a kitten in her lap, Christian and I smiling on.

What I learned from Christian was how to put another human's emotional hat on—empathy versus selfishness. He was in no position to notice my shimmering lure. I was placed in his life to scaffold a fall, to be an ounce of human decency. A position I will recall with great love; I'm proud to say I caused no harm there.

My Autumn with Summer

As sultry August poured in like butterscotch, the neighborhood dahlias, lilies, and zinnias were impossible to resist. I had a pair of clippers in my pocket during every evening walk.

"Reen, you are going to jail," Dani said, as I arranged a huge pile of fugitive flowers and foliage in an assortment of vases on the backyard table.

"It's good for the bush" was always my response. "This neighborhood will miss my great appreciation when we are gone. It will be lonely without my skilled pruning, love, and attention."

I felt Dani's arms from behind wrap around my waist, her thumbs landing on the rim of my front jeans pockets. Resting her head on my back, she breathed me in. We were both acutely aware that within weeks, Jim Cooper would return and our bungalow summer would be over. She had spent hours on her tablet scrolling through real estate properties in the foothills that she might buy. "Maybe next spring," she assured me. "We've got to get you secured in your home, first."

Of the limitless affirmations Dani brought to the table of our alliance, the notion that I had the capacity to support myself was by far the most grandiose. With the monthly mortgage payments over four thousand dollars, I was certain I could not move home without the support of a man.

"Yes, you can. I'll be with you and we'll rent out the downstairs."

As frightened as I was, I had let my renters, the Snake Boyz, know that the time had come. They were international filmmakers. Moving was almost impossible for them, because they were always traveling. We worked out a deal that they could stay a few more months. Dani would stay with another girlfriend who had just bought a ranch and needed some help, and I would find a room somewhere else.

"What about your friend, Summer?" Dani suggested. "Her kids have launched and she is alone."

Dani and I had become a dazzling display of flying squirrels, high-fiving each other in midair as we catapulted from one branch to the next. Even in flight, our incubator of ideas somehow kept us safe from homelessness.

"Hey, that's a brilliant idea," I said. "I'll reach out to her."

Summer was a breeze of a woman, ten years younger than I was, with the rhythm of a soul train dancer. She'd fall into a Baptist trance whenever music took over her, twisting, gyrating, and pounding on her seated drum apparatus.

I'd met her when she was the president of our village business association many years back, and our friendship had unfolded to reveal a kaleidoscope of qualities and interests that put her in the valuable women category.

She had brought me on as photographer for a nonprofit specializing in foster children that allowed me to document the lives of many altruistic families, showing me the necessities of a village in raising a family.

Summer was also a banker, striving to move large institutions into green and responsible investing. I became the photographer for all of her business network. If that weren't enough, from her house, not far from my original home, she boarded dogs and traveling musicians, and had frequent house concerts.

"I am a promoter of good vibes," she had explained.

Her coloring did not match her name; she wore all the shades of grey to suit a passionate, and sometimes stormy, soul. A survivor of cancer, and recently, a sudden and bewildering divorce, I felt compelled to be near her and learn from her.

May I come over?

Sure.

I entered her front gate, securing it behind me so as not to let any dogs out. Most days there were two or three dogs boarding, thus, she had a chamber system of fencing to keep them safe. On this day, she had a vigorous Labrador and her own Ema. Probably not older than eight years, Summer's Coonhound had suffered a stroke, rendering her forever crooked. It was difficult for Ema to walk without the aid of wheels, and getting up from a lying position was painful to watch. We all loved Ema with a fervor for her bravery and resilience. Her tender, dark eyes were a salve for any self-pity, reminding us that we are all a little bit broken, and isn't that all right?

I'd been enjoying my collection of accessories accumulated for the Goddess Project; this day, I had on a large leather scabbard buckled around my waist and right thigh. Where my sword was to go, I holstered an oyster shucker and my cell phone.

"I love you, Reenie," said Summer with a smile, as I entered her living room and she admired my armor.

"It's empowering. You must try it," I said, removing the baldric and buckling it around her waist.

"It does feel great." She catwalked up and down her living room, head held high, landing in a Joan of Arc pose. "How is the project going?"

"It's going slowly, but that's okay. It's the process, not the product. It brings so much pleasure to everyone involved. It's expensive, so I can't rush through it."

It was a warm day, and Summer was wearing shorts and a loose-fitting tank top. I'd never noticed the large tattoo covering her back, shoulder-to-shoulder. "That's just like her," I mused. "Summer, the tattooed banker."

"Would you like a beer?" she said breezily. Opening the fridge, she grabbed two bottles with one hand. "Let's go outside."

The backyard was set up to entertain. A ping-pong game and two large picnic tables sat on one terrace and a tan bark path led to a firepit, with several chairs encircling it. I had spent many evenings around that firepit, guitar in hand, singing with groups of friends. Astride the pit was a structure named the "Brick House," where two sofa beds could open to accommodate up to four guests. Intended for musicians, the Brick House featured a full drum set, several mic stands, and recording equipment.

"I'm in a pickle," I said, sitting down at the picnic table. "I have to be out of Jim's at the end of the month. I have told the Snake Boyz that I'm moving home, but they need more time, maybe a few months. Would you consider renting me the Brick House for a stint?"

Summer peeled the label off her beer, then reached down to stroke Ema, whose chin had landed on her thigh. "I want to leave the Brick House open for musicians, but you could stay in my daughter's old room. I honestly think it's got the best view in the house."

I followed her up into the house and up the stairs to a tiny room overlooking the hills.

"Oh, Summer, it's perfect. I don't know how to thank you. I will call it 'The Turret,' because it's the top of the castle."

From The Turret, I saw my familiar village with a different flexion than I'd known. The valley of homes spread near and far was a comfort. Taking in the tall willows astride carefully managed rose bushes, I could hear the chatter of easy neighbors gathering around barbecues. I was almost home.

She looked into my eyes as if to take in this new beginning. "You will be my wing-woman."

A few weeks later, Dani and I moved most of our things into Jim's garage. He had graciously allowed us to use it for storage until we were to land at my house. I brought with me a garment rack, some clothing, my guitar, Cuisinart, and my fortitude.

I was still hooked on Christian. Letting go of that man was a diet I could not stay on. By buying expensive concert tickets and making elaborate picnics, I could coax him to join me on outings, but he was fading. He needed to work on himself.

"A wall went up," he explained to me one afternoon. "I'm afraid it's time I tell you that we are never going to be a thing."

We hadn't been intimate in weeks, though I still was a recipient of his enveloping bear hugs.

"There's something wrong with that guy," Scoundrel said, admonishing me one afternoon in the studio.

"Well, there's nothing wrong with his thighs," I teased, reminding Mike of the fact that he was not a man of great stature.

"What kind of an idiot would not want to make love to your tits?"

It was endearing how we bantered through our civility. He did have a point, though.

"It's a crush, Mike. It hurts."

I wanted nothing more than handsome Christian to be a sturdy lover and partner, but what I wanted was just not available.

"If you gave half of the energy you put into Christian into your business, you'd be on fire." Summer leaned on the doorframe of my turret. I'd taken to sleeping in my clothes on piles of scarves, shoes, and paperwork now. I was an emotional wreck.

On the wall of my tiny turret hung an eleven-by-fourteen framed print of Christian. I had brought a film camera to the river with me when things were lofty between us. I gazed up at it, studying it for clues of what went wrong.

I had been so high back then, I'd returned to my passion of film-shooting and fine printing. With joy in my heart, I had lovingly printed several fiber-based pieces in the darkroom. I'd made a powerful image of Summer at the Women's March, found old negatives of Dani's sons when they were babies and framed those for her. When I'm in love, my art is on full throttle.

Letting out an exasperated sigh, Summer reached up and lifted the frame from its nail and stormed out of the room.

"Wait! What are you doing?" I sat up in the tiny, cluttered twin bed, knocking my laptop off it.

I could hear Summer ruffling around in her closet down the hall, her motions angry and manic like a deranged racoon. She shouted from her room, "Would you give me a fucking shred of a fucking break?!"

I knew she was hiding my portrait of Christian. Then, downstairs she thundered and returned with my guitar.

"Here!" she thrust my instrument at me. "You're doing this all wrong!" Her anger was palpable. "Don't you get it? You don't stop making art when you are broken, that's when you begin."

As she choked out her words, her face twisted in misery. For an instant, I thought she had stopped breathing, then she surrendered to a spasm of tears. I stood up just in time to soften the blow of her body as she crumpled.

Resting on the floor on a pile of disheveled hats, she inhaled her snotty nose and wiped her eyes with her palms. Recovering with a half-hearted smile, she continued, "You are stronger than this, Reenie."

Summer's tenacity the past several weeks had been dazzling. Up at the crack of dawn, laundry done by 7:00 a.m., she was a wonder to behold. She ran her multiple occupations and household like a commander-in-chief, calling in subcontractors to assist with logos and marketing strategies. With all the accoutrements consummately organized, she could snap multiple carabiners onto her belt loop, and orchestrate six dogs at once, her fabulous hiney sashaying down the trail. She knew her shit. She was fluid, save one area.

After over twenty years of marriage, Bob had left and nobody knew why. The rug had been pulled out from under my friend. The pain must have been unbearably confusing.

I suddenly felt incredibly selfish.

Summer was right. Art is definitely how you get through, and, yes, I could do this. We both had much bigger fish to fry than some guy changing his mind about hitching his wagon to our respective, radiant stars. Like so many others, this glittery, tattered soul had been placed before me by providence as a guide.

Resolvedly, we stood and made counsel in a long and comforting hug. I felt the familiar chocolate syrup of grace come over me and thanked my friend, my God, and the universe, for another pearl.

There was to be a wedding in Arkansas. My cherished childhood friend, Kim, had, like me, spawned a perfect likeness of herself. Mary was planning an autumn wedding on an enormous cattle ranch and I was asked to photograph it. An opportunity for me to get lost.

"I have a cousin in Kansas that I'd like to visit," I explained to Summer, while we sat over morning coffee in our bathrobes, "and one of my basketball celebrities was traded to one of those flat states: Indiana, I think. Maybe I could reach out to his wife and see if she wants me to photograph a day-in-the-life piece on her family."

"Well, that sounds interesting." She smiled assuredly, like a mother setting a daughter adrift on a whim.

Kansas, Arkansas, and Indiana felt far away. Far from the garden I had planted in Summer's manicured yard, far from the comfort of sweet Ema. But most importantly, far from Christian.

"I'll just drive," I bolstered, waving my hand to the distance, "due east."

"You're the worst driver in the world." Summer pursed her lips. "I'd think this would be quite a challenge for you."

"Exactly," I responded.

In August, white-supremacist and neo-Nazi protesters held a Unite the Right rally in Charlottesville, Virginia. The marchers chanted racist and anti-Semitic slogans, carrying weapons and anti-Semitic flags. One of the protesters, James Alex Fields Jr., deliberately rammed his car into a crowd of counter-protesters, killing one woman and injuring nineteen other people.

President Trump's remarks, "very fine people on both sides," were seen by critics as implying moral equivalence between the white-supremacist marchers and those who protested against them. Some interpreted his remarks as sympathetic to white supremacists, causing the resignation of several CEOs, including the heads of Campbell Soup, Intel, Merck, Under Armour, and 3M, and the presidents of Alliance for American Manufacturing, and the AFL-CIO, not to mention seventeen members of the White House arts and humanities advisory panel. Trump called the reaction grandstanding.

Then there were threats to shut down the federal government if Congress refused to allocate funds for Trump's "Mexican wall" policy. A presidential pardon was granted for Sheriff Joe Arpaio, who was convicted of criminal contempt in a case involving his department's racial-profiling policy, praising Arpaio's life work in protecting the public from crime and illegal immigration. If that weren't enough, our President signed an executive order to restore the flow of surplus military equipment to local and state police agencies.

Kansas

The sun was just peeking out with a florid glimmer on the western horizon as I loaded my camera gear and knapsack into the back of Summer's Jeep for a lift to the airport. I'd decided I would fly to Kansas and make the rest of the trip via rental car. I hadn't told Christian about my plan to run away. I was looking forward to exploring the Midwest whilst discovering what I might do if left entirely to my own devices. I wished to report to nobody.

First stop, Manhattan, Kansas, also known as "the little apple." My cousin, Charlie, had moved from his home in Seattle to head the linguistics department at Kansas State University. Charlie and his wife, Hazel, were lively and perspicacious. A wholly balanced family, they'd sired two young, scarlet-haired daughters, the kind that run into your arms. Like most voyagers of Europe, they were of the belief that summer was a holiday, and frequently visited family in Seattle and San Francisco during that time, including having a stay with me (back when I'd had a home).

Charlie was the second son of my mother's sister. We'd had numerous childhood summers under our belts. Being near him beckoned wieldy memories as soothing as a red station wagon. Charlie was shocked when I phoned to ask if I could visit him in Kansas, a part of the Midwest that wasn't always the first choice of tourists.

"Well, Noreen," he'd said, putting on his best imitation of Grandpa, "we would be delighted to host you in our little apple."

Kansas has fireflies, or lightnin' bugs as they've been coined there. Call them whatever you want. As far as I'm concerned, they are ineffable. We sat on the porch of Charlie and Hazel's 1914 craftsman home. On either side of me, on the wicker porch swing, nuzzled my extended heart in the shape of "nieces," one under each arm. They'd been fighting all day to sit next to me in the car, to hold my hand on the long, colorful prairie we had explored. Looking up at the rolling patchwork of wildflowers, I'd expected a tiny Laura Ingalls to stumble down the mountain in her calico pinafore and bonnet, lunch-bucket and belted books in hand. These little girls were family.

It had been a warm and balmy day of adventure followed by a block party put on by the neighbors. Corn and casseroles were passed around a table of genuine, homespun characters. I wondered if any of these women thought it necessary to depilate their nether regions, but held my tongue during mealtime.

As the girls started to doze off, Charlie instructed them to tend to teeth and pajama duties, to which they gave little protest, feeling ready to sleep. He stood up and ferried them into the house.

"Hazel?" I asked easily, as if I were asking her to pass the salt, "do you shave your vagina?"

My cousin-in-law brought both hands to her hairline from forehead to ear and stroking her scalp, skillfully pulled her mop of curls into a ponytail. Tying it in a knot, she had an instant bun without a band or clip. Her red ringlets were like currency, her daughters being heir to her natural riches.

"I did, once."

This, throughout my random-yet-comprehensive survey, seemed to be the most common answer. "What would it be like," so many women ventured, "to be clean-shaven? Would intercourse be more pleasurable? Would I swim faster? Would I be more attractive?"

"I looked like a plucked chicken and the grow-back was ridiculous. I'll never do it again. I did it as a surprise for Charlie's birthday and he hardly even noticed."

Charlie emerged from the house with a cold bottle of white wine in one hand and three glasses in the other, signaling a query with an arch of a brow.

As he sat down to join us, Hazel continued, "That's kind of out of the blue." Then, turning to her husband, she said, "Your cousin just asked me if I shave my pubic hair."

"Well, sweetie pie!" he purred, again, an imitation of Grandpa. "It's all the same to me!"

Charlie stood to make a formality of opening the wine. Pouring just an inch into one goblet he lifted it toward the rising moon to carefully scrutinize the viscosity and color. Then, bringing the glass to his nose, he closed his eyes and inhaled contemplatively for a full ten seconds.

"Honeysuckle," he exhaled euphorically. "Melon, fresh clover." Then bringing his glass to his lips, he took the whole swill in his mouth and swished loudly. With an audible swallow, his eyes sprung open with an epiphany, and raising his glass, he announced, "This wine is as sweet as the choice rose of my wife's pubis!"

We clapped our hands in delight.

Leaving that family to drive east was difficult. My knapsack packed with drawings and special rocks from our long weekend together would serve as souvenirs. This seemed to bring consolation. Of course, I'd had my camera, which always softens the haste of change.

"The next time I see you," I said, smirking at the girls, "you will have grown. That's why I'm glad I got to see you now." Planting a seed that they are a part of something bigger—the *us*, was my intent.

As I pulled away in my rental car, I watched my little Kansas family waving behind me and smiled a teary goodbye. "What a great family my grandparents had created for us all," I thought as I respired. "How did they do that? And where on earth do I find a Charlie of my very own?"

A seven-hour drive affords time to think. It was very warm crossing the prairie lined with limitless fields of hay rolls perched on their sides like cinnamon buns. I didn't know where I was and I reveled in the feeling. I knew I wouldn't arrive in Arkansas until after dark, but I put the fear of driving on autopilot, enjoying the vast country. Knowing the trip would be a long one, well over five hundred miles, I took time to reflect on what

I had learned about all these men and women I had spent time with over the past year, and where my experiences had placed me.

I had interviewed scores of women on the subject of the *hair de nethers*. Deeming it about as unimportant as a hairstyle, each expressed an individual preference: long, short, bald, partial, and all for different reasons. Bringing up the subject always brought me closer to the person with whom I spoke. First aghast by the query, each and every gal opened up to the opportunity to share. Our divine center, in general, is an area where women should commune. It unites us. Never once did I regret bringing it up.

Mine never came back after cancer.
I just like to be clean-shaven.
My guy likes a landing strip.
I wax the whole dang thing.
Waxing is too expensive.
I get more action clean-shaven.
I gave up after I got married.
My husband asked me to and I told him to go to hell.

One young girl in Alice's crowd was veritably famous for not depilating at all. Known as a kind of Frida Khalo of the gang, young men sought her out, compelled by her bravery. She became a fetish of sorts.

"So I smell like fish," she'd shrugged. "Don't all mermaids smell like fish?"

It had been while having lunch with my son and his housemate at a glorious winery surrounded by rose gardens that Henry asked me to explain my study of *les cheveux du vagin* to his buddy.

"I'm fascinated by the changing trend. The misconception that vaginal hair is unsanitary brings us back to the era of douching with Lysol. The hair has a purpose, like an eyebrow."

I further waxed on the work of Peggy Orenstein, a contemporary writer, who always seemed to have her pen on my concerns. In *Girls and Sex*, she noted that eighty percent of young women were going Brazilian and wondered why. Fashion, coercion, or comfort?

Henry's friend was married, with a new baby. A beautiful man with thick, black, shoulder-length hair and a wonderful moustache above perfectly puffy lips.

"I shave," he quipped, "everything. It's something nice I can do for my wife."

Remembering this, hands ten-and-two on the turnpike, I laughed. What a sweet guy, who had so easily softened the edges of my unimportant, snarky feminist survey. Why not wear all of your hair in a fashion that most pleases your lover?

I wished I had one of those: a lover.

After stopping for gas and pistachios, I opted for an audiobook I'd stored that brought comfort to my beleaguerment. Ali Binazir's *The Tao of Dating* was one I'd heard before, yet often reached for when craving wisdom. Alex, he likes to call himself, is a prophet that understands the exact same principle as *The Artist's Way*, my sister's teachers, and well, pretty much all common sense of the universe.

"You are complete as you are, girl," his voice focused on me, in my rented blue Ford Fusion.

"I know," I reminded myself. "But my heart is hurting."

Alex went on to explain why we wasted our time on shitty men and simply laid out what a good guy was. A good guy seeks out truth, has a sense of purpose, allows for humility, and makes decisions. A good man is trustworthy, considerate, and has a strong internal compass. He embraces equanimity, is graceful under pressure, and is accepting of life as it rolls.

I took in Ali's words, and recapped my recent adventures. Perhaps, although I thought I was taking care of myself, I really was wasting a great deal of time dating, and should instead go back to my Goddess Project, my home, and my garden. Maybe it wasn't a guy I was needing.

Cowboys

When I arrived in Arkansas, it was dark. Kim welcomed me with open arms. Not the Kim named after a vaginal wig, but the Kim from my childhood. When I say childhood, I practically mean toddlerhood. In second grade, I was immediately attracted to her puppy-like pigtails, broad lips, and adventurous smile, plus her dad had a camper. We were crossing guards together, and, as she lived a short walk up the hill, our friendship was easy and steady, demonstrated by our matching silver engraved bracelets. It was Kim there in the field reading porn, it was she at the basement party where I lost my virginity. When my father took his life, it was she who showed up at my tiny apartment with a suitcase, saying, "You are not going to do this alone."

Kim holds the largest swath of color in my shawl, and although, much to all of our chagrin, she married a cowboy and moved to Arkansas, we were on the phone for hours at least three times a week.

"I can't believe you did this. Thank you." Green eyes on blue, she charged down the front stairs to help me unpack. Some things change, like the now loose folds under our chins and the texture of our skin around our eyes and mouth, yet some things endure like this abiding soul of navigation through any current. A treasured ally.

I was there for two reasons: to stop thinking about Christian and to shoot Mary's wedding. Mary's likeness to her mother was prodigious, like it was with my Alice, and being near her was a delightful *déjà vu* of our youth. We had twinkled like crystal and pennies in our days. Two hot girls on hot summer nights.

"I cannot think of anything I would rather do," I said, surveying the new house I had not yet known beyond descriptions and cell phone images.

It was quaint, with a bric-a-brac kitchen motif and charming country accoutrements. "Just promise me she is marrying the right guy."

Twenty-five years earlier, Kim had married J.D., short for "Just Drinkin'," in my backyard on Snake Road, where she donned my wedding dress. He was sexy, and trouble from the start. Informing her he was to be a fireman, he tore my best friend from me and her precious parents and siblings, dragging her to the far, flat state of Arkansas. A constant disappointment, J.D. had her on a farm a hundred miles from the nearest Walmart and her work as a dental hygienist. Coming from a Ward and June Cleaver household, she'd been blindsided after fifteen years of marriage, when the news broke that he had slept with not one, but thirty-seven women in the neighboring county.

Her girls, Lily-Grace and Mary-Paige, were the silver lining of this storm. I'd come out ten years earlier to play with them on the farm for a few weeks. We'd bought goats, made Easter bonnets, and planted a garden. On the occasional Christmas, they would scrape up enough to fly out to California for a holiday with Kim's family. I would photograph them in my studio, so we could all have images to lean into, softening the painful absence of their rapidly growing bodies. J.D. never came.

Kim was our democratic plant in a red state. We would talk for hours as she described the bucolic folks around her. Once, I mailed her some artichokes, and as she sat in the park enjoying one, children gathered around her and asked, "Is that what an avocado looks like?" It would be impossible for my soul mate to come back to California, due to the ties of the girls, who were firmly planted in the Midwest. So, she started chewing gum and opted to bloom where she was planted.

"Cyler is a gem." Kim set a plate of chicken potpie before me. "He's a teacher and a baseball coach over in Missouri. As soon as Mary gets her nursing credentials, they will buy a little house. Most importantly, he thinks our girl hung the moon. You'll meet him tomorrow when you survey the wedding site. We'll go right after breakfast. You won't believe it, Reen. It's where they do the chuck-wagon races."

The following morning, we drove a short seven miles through the Ozark foothills. The last mile, on a gravelly road, proved to be the driveway to a colossal ranch. Perched high above a cavernous, alluvial riverbed, there were several acres of grass just perfect for a wedding. A large, airy, antler-covered ranch house, a guesthouse, barn, and pavilion were spread over the property. It was my job to decide where the light would be best for the ceremony.

I was metering under an ancient oak tree, when the owner of the ranch, Mick, screeched up the mountain path entrance in a white F10 pickup, followed by several dogs of various sizes and stages of health. In these parts, an F10 is considered a compact vehicle, and a three-legged dog is as common as wild buttercup.

"Smile to release endorphins." Kim clenched, then with a whole body wave, put on her southern drawl. "Hey Mick, I want you to meet our *photographer.*"

Out of the cab emerged a beautiful specimen of a man, probably sixty. With silver hair and a long, matching handlebar moustache, he was wearing, despite the balmy morning, a checkered button-up with leather-trimmed breast pockets, mother-of-pearl snaps, a large, silver belt buckle embossed with a longhorn steer, and, naturally, a ten-gallon hat. He extended his calloused hand, and when I offered mine, I felt immediately protected and unsettled at the same time.

"All the way from California, I hear," said Mick, not slowing from the work at hand.

Circling to the back of the truck, I observed the two-foot "TRUMP" sticker on his tailgate before he lowered it to drag out a very large box of Tide, or rather a Tide box filled with some kind of treat for the dogs, the incessant barking being my indicator. One by one, he began hurling handfuls of some kind of meat on the grass, which the dogs hungrily fought

over. I was trying to make out what the byproduct was when Mick's wife
appeared on a red riding mower.

"Hey Mick, did you get them steers castrated?"

"Testicles," Kim mouthed to me.

Patty, Mick's wife, was an equally sturdy woman. One of those "just
about the nicest gals you'd ever want to meet," she immediately stepped
in to show us around the place. Before leaving the truck, though, I had to
get one in.

"Hey Mick, I have a great recipe for braised mountain oysters, if you'd
ever like to try them."

Mick stopped, removed his hat, and after looking me up and down,
cocked his head and winked. "I'll jes' bet you do."

The following morning, we were all set up. The girls were at the local
hair salon having their hair ratted into impervious-to-weather pageant helmets and enduring the installation of false eyelashes. The unattended
flower girl and ring bearer were splashing about in the pedicure basin and
I was documenting it all. My viewfinder caught Mary in her chair, and I
zoomed in to take a closer look. Snapping a frame, I inspected the image.
The light was divine on her expression as she looked off into her future.
Her chiseled lips, a perfect likeness to my best friend's, reminded me of
the times when we would turn each other upside down, draw eyes and a
nose on our chins, and make puppets of our lips, frowning to look like a
smile. A deep and familiar love *twinged* my body in a light sweat, and my
heart recited my prayer: "Cyler, you hurt a single hair on this girl's head
and I swear I will come down here and personally remove your heart with
a Bowie knife."

Looking up, I noticed that Kim was watching me with a trusting expression. Her hair was starting to look like Loretta Lynn's, with ringlets
coming out of nowhere in the back.

When our eyes met, she breathed in deeply to balance herself. "J.D.'s
here," she said with an exhale.

"But I thought he didn't want to partici—"

"But, he's J.D."

My focus moved from Kim to the distance behind her and found J.D.
leaning against the wall, surveying the salon like it was a harem. Tall and
broad-shouldered, no one could fill out a shirt like J.D., even at fifty-five.

Wow, I hadn't seen him since, *gosh*, since we bought goats together. Of
course, he was Mary's father. Of course, he'd be there and turn out to be

the hero, tossing Bud Lights to the groomsmen while they dressed in the barn.

After all these years, J.D. was still compelling, a trait that nature had misappropriated, or somewhere, someone had let this could-a-been-a-great-man down to the point of no repair.

The wedding could not have been finer. Mary-Paige was as radiant as the late summer light, while God blessed the union of what was clearly a perfect bond. They drove away in a 1947 Dodge truck, and Kim and I danced to "100 Years," by Five for Fighting.

We'd been invited to stay in the big house and had been granted the whole place to ourselves. After the last of the guests left, Kim opened her first beer and peeled off her tight chemise. Kicking off her painful shoes, she moaned. "Let's swim!"

Outside the sliding glass door, looking over the starry precipice, the sky stretched in wispy watercolors of orange and magenta morphing to purple. Off in the distance, we could hear the cattle lowing as we sculled, belly-up, in the quiet swimming pool, something we had both mastered at sleepover camp decades ago. My ears underwater, I felt the familiar comfort of the womb, aside the echoing sound of Kim's laughter. I lifted my head. "What?"

"Did you see fucking John Duke talking to my dad? My poor dad doesn't know what to make of him."

"Nobody knows what to make of him," I said.

Just then, the front doorbell chimed. Kim got out of the pool, wrapped a towel around herself, and disappeared toward the door. I couldn't see, but could hear the familiar drawl of the offensive man who had ruined my friend's life.

"Anyone here feelin' ready fer a nightcap?" As J.D. imposed himself through the house and onto the patio, he noticed me in the pool and tipped his hat using the bottle neck of a half-full handle of Jim Beam.

"I'll jes' find us some glasses," he asserted.

As he turned into the kitchen, I made my escape out of the pool and into a nearby bedroom to dress.

Kim could handle this. She always had in the past, with her tool belt of family fortitude. I could hide in a bedroom far away and wait. When I felt strong enough, I emerged in sweatpants and a T-shirt.

There, to my amazement, I found the two of them sitting on the edge of the pool, Kim's feet wading in the dark, cool water as they talked and laughed together.

As if nothing had happened all these years, as if he had no memory of the hell he had imposed, the misery and poverty he'd inflicted on his family, J.D. pulled off his boots, rolled up his blue jeans, and dipped his feet in the pool astride Kim's.

I couldn't hear what they were saying. My friend was smiling. I had no interest in joining them, so I found myself a chaise with a view of the forever-wide canyon under the starry dome to ponder the day's activities and the people I had met while documenting the day.

Cowboys, I mused, are a strange breed. Harlons, Earls, and Roys, they are raised to do hard work and hide their tears. Respecting women was a frequent farce, but if you were to peel off the hard crust, you'd most likely find a little boy in there, craving the acceptance of the feminine. These men would never allow you to carry anything heavier than a tray of food, coming to your rescue should a table or bale of hay be in need of reconfiguration. Making women feel attractive is taught early. On several occasions, I felt a twinge of the animal sexuality swirling around the party. I couldn't rest an opinion on it, but the term that came to mind was "provisional," not meaning temporary, rather, capable of providing goods and services. I do like a man who can bring his abilities and a freshly butchered chicken to the table.

Hearing a scuttle like a fox in a henhouse, I turned around. J.D. was rushing out, quickly grabbing his hat and carrying his boots. "Shore was nice to see you, Noreen." He flashed a Sundance-kid grin at me.

I swiveled my gaze to Kim for an explanation. By the expression on her face, it would have been appropriate if she'd had a broom in her hand.

"Was it nice catching up with J.D.?"

"Motherfucker!" she spit. "I'd expect no less from him. He asked me for a blow job!"

September limped away as we watched hurricanes Harvey and Irma tear apart the south and Puerto Rico.

President Trump terminated Obama's DACA program designed to shield from deportation undocumented immigrants who came to the US as children. And, why not? After a rally in Charlottesville run by white nationalists, white supremacists, the Ku Klux Klan, neo-Nazis, and other hate groups, our fair leader argued that both sides were at fault.

I, though, was gearing up to move home, yes, *home*. While summering with Dani, knowing that the move was imminent, I had planted hundreds of sunflowers from seed in transportable flats. I'd also ordered a half-dozen baby chicks and feathered them out in a brooder box on the patio. I was distressed that I hadn't found my new love to take care of me, Goddess knows that I'd tried. I had found a much more interesting answer deep in my heart. A stronger scaffolding could not be imaginable. A love of immense strength, impervious to damage and pain. One that I could count on, and after this arduous adventure, know intimately and authentically. My own self.

Before leaving for my southeastern journey, Dani had helped me move the then-teenaged chickens into the coop and gently install the seedlings into the garden.

"I'm so proud of you, Reen." Dani's eyes softened.

She watched as I carefully cupped each tiny plant into the soil I'd prepared. Just then, the balcony door, the one leading off what was, and would be again, my bedroom, opened up. Vinnie, one of the filmmakers who had skippered this ship of a house while I was on my heart sabbatical for the past six years, stepped out.

"Hey, Reen!" Vin was young and strong, a genuine Italian in his early thirties. "So, we have to care for these chickens and garden?"

"Yes, I'll show you how."

The transition was clear. I'd given the Snake Boyz several months' notice that it was time for me to come home, support system or not, and I wanted it to be plumb upon my return. They'd secured living arrangements elsewhere. Our tenant-owner relationship was coming to an end. I had loved these young guys, who produced astounding work, and often thought that it would be so nice just to disappear so that they could stay. But they didn't want to live with me and I needed to come home. It was time.

"Come in," Vinnie said, motioning toward me.

My house, waiting for me for so many years, was still mine. I stood on the patio and contemplated the view. As wide as my arms could spread, I could witness a view of the San Francisco Bay. I could remember planting the children's placentas under each fruit tree. I could recall every piece of antique furniture handed down from my parents, and the solid stories that went with each.

"This piece," I could almost hear mother's voice, "is from the Jacobean era."

Vinnie and I hugged before I left. "I'll be back in a few months."

How to Teach Your Son Not to Be a Rapist

As we turned the corner on our newest feminine growing pains, the #Me-Too Movement emerged. Men of power, celebrities, coaches, movie directors, etc., were dropping like pine needles from a beetle-infested conifer. Women were coming out of the paneling with allegations of having been inappropriately harassed by men. The news cavalcaded through the media, beginning with Harvey Weinstein, then on down to respected characters like Garrison Keiller, Kevin Spacey, Tom Brokaw, and even my own favorite, Charlie, who ran our local eatery. Over seventy allegations were listed in two months' time, and I wondered, would I say "me, too"?

Naturally, I had been advanced upon frequently throughout my womanhood, but had I missed life opportunities by saying *no*? I understood the game, mirroring animal behavior, like the baboons at the zoo. "Here is my bright, shiny ass. Take it that I might gain a position of power." Yet, we strive to create a just and gentle system of roles that can allow us to still enjoy intimacy, without behaving like baboons. We're always working on equal opportunity and this was a major *kachink*. A cataclysmic shift was happening to open up the conversation. How can we guide our men through this change? Empower women without disempowering our men. These men of power—Bill Cosby, for God's sake—wielded their authority for sex. What can we, as mothers, do to keep our children safe from these trappings?

So, I'm standing in the rain in the parking lot of my local supermarket, trying to maneuver two heavy bags while keeping my cart from rolling away with my hip. One of the flimsy paper handles breaks and as I bend my leg to catch my groceries, I look up to see a young man.

"Good luck with that," he said, smirking. Was he being rancorous, and if so, why? I opted to call him out.

"Hey, there," I frowned, "I could use some help."

His reaction was no surprise. His face relaxed into congeniality, as he rushed to my rescue and took hold of both of the bags with ease.

"Of course," he said. "I'm sorry."

Men are fragile and beautiful creatures. A development that I configured myself several times over as a mother. They are a direct product of what we put in. From countless hours of singing in that rocking chair to every learned skill, craft, and design. Holding them closely when Little League left them behind, the guidance, arguments, separation, and *The Runaway Bunny*. "We don't throw mud clots at passing cars, my love." Parents guide these forming brains. Social mores and depictions of the roles between men and women have often shown women as the weaker sex, but we all know that is bullshit. We needn't be accusatory or cruel to men, just firm: "not cool, buddy."

This guy was afraid I was going to call his assistance an admission of my weakness. So, let's unpack this.

Guidance. Boundaries. Rules. Rewards. It works for children; it works for men. Another way to put it, to add to Anne Lamott's wisdom: *Help, Thanks, Wow, Here.* Guys want acceptance as much as they want sex. (Well, so do I.) We can teach our boys how to act consensually and how to read the road map and enjoy the trip of love.

When my boys were teenagers, I'd put in their Christmas stockings a tiny Victorian booklet, *The Gentlemen's Book of Etiquette*. Though absurdly archaic, they actually read the damn thing. Perhaps today's men don't need to be equipped with tools, such as which fork to use or which side of the street to walk on when in the company of a lady, but having a full wheelhouse of quintessential behaviors can provide solid resources that can be called upon in times of confusion. When entering a party, always greet the host and hostess. Always send a thank-you note.

I don't believe that today's emancipated woman feels belittled when a door is opened or a hat, tipped. I do, however, believe that we have no room for brute force, coercion, or manipulation. A suitcase of simple acceptable manners can go far, but a tiny manual of manners from the 1860s does not alone suffice.

This brings me to the subject of "Guys with Good Dads." Boys model what they witness. If their fathers are kind and attentive to their mothers, it's more likely that they will behave similarly. There are many chains to break, and the #MeToo Movement has helped bring this awareness to the forefront.

When I heard the catch phrase, "toxic masculinity," I felt instantly protective of my boys, so I asked some questions.

"Men are not toxic," my daughter explained, "the roles our society feeds them are."

I could see all of the ways we had let our boys down. Traditional roles depict men as aggressive, competitive, and power-seeking, lacking empathy and vulnerability. The media shows women as sex objects to conquer. If left to their own devices, to learn only from fraternities and pornography, they will be unguided, and, well, dickheads. Our paradigm is upside down. Rather than teaching our girls how not to get raped, what if we teach our sons how not to be rapists?

Testosterone is stunning and sexy, and most importantly, useful. This magnificent hormone causes a mate to be protective, resourceful, strong, and able to open pickle jars and reach things. The oh-so-important sex confabulation is not just one conversation, it's an ongoing dialogue.

"All of the fire, all of the rivers, all of the flowers and all of the world is waiting for you to grow into a man" is my intended message. It's important to encourage the positive qualities of being a man.

"You are good at fixing things. I like that you are there for your friends. A healthy relationship with your partner is nourishing. Consensual sex is sexy. And I think it is absolutely paramount that there be conversations clearly and frequently around pornography.

"Funny how you rarely see faces, smiles, or kisses, isn't it? Does it look like these women are cherished? Masturbation is healthy, and a good place to start, but be super-duper careful what brings you satisfaction."

I mused on all of these men I had been learning about on this path. I gathered them all into my heart like flowers in a bouquet and pinned my heart on each and every one of them. Maybe I would never find him, or conceivably I had, over and over.

Salubrious

October and November blurred by. As the weather turned bright orange with the smell of pending football games and bright autumn foliage, Dani and I worked ardently on feathering our new nest.

My home.

I had told the Snake Boyz to use any of my furniture but to utilize the basement when something was in their way. Of course, mother's china had no place in their millennial landscape, as well as several pieces of art, books, candlesticks, and the like.

Straddling a coffee table that they had somehow managed to cram into the cold, spider-and-rat-infested cellar, I twisted and wrestled out a large box and set it on the ground.

"Here, Dani. Flash the light over here." On the box, scrawled in black Sharpie, read the words "Reen's home pix albums."

"Oh no, girl," Dani cautioned. "You've hit an obstacle. This is going to put a wrench in our progress."

"Come on," I prevailed. "We have to stop for lunch, anyway. Aren't you hungry?"

It required both of us to heave the box up, but rather than set it in the pile of things we had conspired to find a place for, we set in on the kitchen counter to examine immediately.

"Dive on in, Reen." Dani smiled as she bent low in front of the refrigerator and extracted the previous evening's leftovers, chicken adobo and rice.

The first album was a watercolor sketchbook that I had filled with early black-and-white prints I had made in a darkroom. Applied via spraymount, the pages were brittle and aromatic. There we were, Stephan and I standing on joists, mid-remodel. We were painfully thin, tanned, and wiry. I, in braids, Steph in a headband to hold back his shoulder-length, unkempt tresses. A cross-parody of the King James' version of Jesus in Levi's and our now-grown son, Henry, Steph's ample tool belt lay low on his hips. I ran my fingers across the heavy fiber print, now rippled with age, and landed on his long torso.

"God, I loved him." I whimpered.

"We're not doing this, Reen." Dani set a warmed plate in front of me.

"Yes, we are." I folded my legs up into my chair. "I want to. Wilma wants me to."

The original builder of my home was a communist lesbian woman in 1940 named Wilma Lloyd. She'd long since passed when we'd purchased the house in 1987, leaving delicious clues to pique my historical hunger. I'd been obsessed with her, happening upon her presence in the form of exotic corms and bulbs busting out in the rock garden, announcing the arrival of spring. Special hiding places deep inside cubbies and walls revealed her communist literature, newspapers, cosmopolitan magazines, and even a stale box of chocolates, probably received from a caller. Wilma was the spiritual guardian of whoever inhabited the house. I'd been gone for six years and felt the need for some kind of ritual to let her apparition know that I was home.

We pored over hundreds of images, all recordings of my life in this house. Marriages and births, toddlers and music, tantrums and teenagers. The furniture in these pictures was younger, more vibrant than what had remained.

"But it's all still here," I marveled. "This house remains strong. The very symbol of my resilience."

We harvested a handful of prints depicting my family's history and pinned them on a bulletin board as a reminder, then moved on to the tasks at hand. The garden would need a do-over, art would need to be reinstalled, and Dani and I would need to settle into this big and breezy house.

Fifteen of the San Francisco 49ers took a knee during the national anthem in October in observance of social and racial injustice. President Trump reinstated North Korea on the list of state-sponsored terrorists as he cozied up next to Putin. He passed huge tax cuts to corporations and continued to ignore subpoenas to show his personal finances. Regardless of clear allegations of sexual misconduct with minors, our President endorsed Alabama State Senator Roy Moore, a strong opponent to same-sex marriage. Yet, Dani and I were busy decorating the house for the holidays.

"What the hell are you doing with those?" Dani gawked as I wrestled in two four-by-eight-foot sheets of three-quarter-inch plywood through the front French doors. At eighteen-by-twenty-four feet, the living room was expansive with over twenty feet of glass opening to sweeping bay views.

"We are going to have the best Salubrious Sunday in the history of Sundays. Come outside with me and help me get some sawhorses."

"We need a guy," Dani asserted, as she buckled under the weight of the wood. We placed the lumber end-to-end on the sawhorses, creating a table long enough for a royal ball.

"We-most-definitely-do-not," I hurled, sliding the davenport to the wall.

After a year of speed-dating, I had finally come to the conclusion that me-and-my-big-self did indeed have the fortitude to stand on my own two feet. I could support myself financially, with the assistance of a tenant or two, and I found myself springing from boulders like a mama lion. I was strong, independent, and could lean on a number of lovers, should I wish to, but I didn't need anyone.

Completely devoid of cynicism, I felt satisfied with the men I had met and learned from.

For the last Salubrious Sunday of my year on OkCupid, I opted to invite as many of the men I had dated that I could locate. Of course, Morgan, the catfisher, could not navigate a trip from Nigeria, but Christian was there, Tony-ssage, Thurston, Errand Boy, Superman, a few that are not mentioned in this book, and naturally, my Scoundrel, who appeared at my door with a glowing pair of kittens, which I named after my mother and father, Bud and Louellyn.

I served several dozen oysters, twelve Dungeness crab, and arugula salad.

Now it was time to continue my Goddess Project.

I wondered if I could photograph myself.

THE END

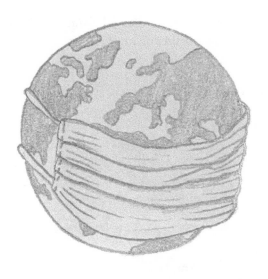

Epilogue

Or alternate ending - you get to choose

As the gentle reader has probably gleaned, this memoir is not completely accurate. What I've claimed transpired over the course of one year, 2017, was, in fact, a four-year development. The first Women's March was indeed in 2017, as was the #MeToo Movement, but many of my important relationships were not a mere three or four weeks. My every intention was to end my story in December 2017. My truth and radiant wisdom being that my need for a man was an illusion, and my brilliant reality being that my true love had been there all along, residing in my own confident heart. But that's too easy.

If I were to be completely authentic with what I learned, we'd have to look back at my return from the south in September, after the trip I took to wash my hair of the crush I'd had on Christian and to photograph sweet Mary's wedding. I hadn't come back transformed into a triumphant

Goddess of self-worth and power, as I'd alluded to. In truth, upon my return, I found my sweet Walter on my doormat.

I couldn't believe it. I couldn't believe it.

> How you doing?

His text hit me like a comet.

> Well, hello. I'm quite well. I have at last moved back into my house after years trying to get here. How are you, Walter?

> I'm better than ever. I wonder if you might want to get together?

Oh My God, Oh My God, Oh My God. I reflected on the few times I had seen Walt over the past two years. Each time, I had somehow handled it with a cool head, allowing him to submerge frequently as he was prone to do.

> I have a place now, and I have a car. No kids this weekend.

> Would you like to have a sleepover? I can turn on the hot tub.

Walter came over, guitar in hand, and played an homage to his divorce, just finalized. He was a sight for sore eyes; I literally ran to the door.

Walter, tall, broad, and sultry, was from Pennsylvania, giving him an east coast feel. He'd attended boarding school, adding a Dead Poets Society flair. I visualized him running to chapel while securing his tie. He'd studied at Tulane, granting a dash of voodoo, and now, an architect, living in the city, his Embarcadero office drove me crazy with desire. He was eloquent, funny, and embraced all things interesting and dodgy without judgement. Things did not bother him. I never once wished he would go home so I could poo or floss or dress. I wanted to be with him always, his white Panama hat perched on my bedside lamp.

He unfurled slowly and cautiously, but after a few short months, he told me that he loved me, and asked if we could go steady.

"Well, let me think about that. Yes!"

We ran to each other every time we saw each other like magnetic silver spoons. Countless weekends were spent either bathing by a fire and loitering in bed all day, or getting lost in Tahoe, the river, or Hawaii. We had absolutely everything in common. Love of the shoreline, French café music, and each other.

"I've written you a song," he said one evening, sitting on a picnic table at Summer's house.

"You have?"

When Walter sang, people listened. He was very gifted, and remarkably handsome. His strumming made obvious his years of dedication.

I met her in a dodgy bar in a cougar jacket and a red beret.
She asked me what I wanted and I told her all I needed was some
  kindness
Oh, oh, my Noreen. With your eyes blazing blue.
Oh, oh, my Noreen. Don't you run away, run away, run away.

Walking into the kitchen, I leaned against the counter to catch my breath. "He really likes you, Reen." Summer followed me in. "I love the way he looks at you."

"I'm sitting perched high on the precipice of an orgasm," I confided. "I guard this love with my life. I honestly think I have never been this kind of happy, ever. Everyone likes him, my family, all my friends. His mother and sister like me. It's too good to be true."

"Let's do it!" I called my esthetician, Stephanie. "The Full Monty."

The following week I was on the table where I usually enjoy facials, glutes in the air, hoping not to fart on dear Stephanie as her face was all up in my business.

"I can't believe you've never done this before. Walter is going to be thrilled. Your lovely parts are going to scream 'love me, touch me, taste me'!"

I felt the warm pressure of hot wax on my tender tushy, which she applied with a tongue depressor. Then skillfully twirling the stick like a caramel apple, said, "now, sit still." With that, she yanked hard on the wax and quickly pushed her palm on the assaulted skin. I almost fainted from the pain. After an excruciating thirty minutes of torture, I looked down, anticipating the porn star of my plan. What I observed was a very angry, very bald eleven-year-old.

"Jesus, Stephanie! Who is this? I look like a baby."

"It'll calm down. Looks like you have a little birthmark right here on the left."

"Put it back, man. Maybe I need to get a merkin."

"You'll get used to it, and Walter will thank me for it."

That evening, I unveiled my surprise to Walt. "*Aw*, you didn't have to do that for me. I love you just the way you are."

I explained that it was an experiment for my writing, but I kind of wished I'd asked first. In two weeks' time, my eleven-year-old turned into a sixteen-year-old with all the hysteria and acne to go with it.

In a short time, Walter introduced me to his kids, then eight and ten. We started slowly, with picnics on the beach, moving on to dinners, then sleepovers. We brought them camping on a river and to a cabin in the snow with my grown kids. I enjoyed playing with them almost as much as I loved to watch Walt father them so beautifully. We brought them to the club to swim and introduced them to my house with its kittens and chickens. One afternoon, I caught his daughter with her chin resting on my dresser, scrutinizing my altar for Rick, with the remarkable watercolor that Molly had made for me when he'd passed.

"Was he nice?" Melody's eyes were almond, with the tiniest strip of translucent shine drawn by God under her lower lashes, like the golden paint on a chrysalis, though hers was silver. This, I believed was from her mother, who was Asian. She and her brother Jack were both a perfect amalgam of their mother and Walter's Swedish/German genes. Every fiber of that little girl wanted a dog, and the stories I would extol about Rick seemed to strengthen her plea.

"The city is no place for a dog."

"I see dogs in the city all the time."

"You don't have a yard."

"I'll walk him."

"But Daddy has to go to work and you have to go to school."

Then, two things happened.

First, Walter found a bigger place with a fenced yard. Having been born in a condo, the kids had only been outside in city parks and playgrounds.

Situated in a sweet turn-of-the-century neighborhood in south San Francisco, the kids each had a private room and Walter's room looked out on a Japanese maple and two lilac shrubs. Upon inspecting the yard, I asked, "May I garden here?"

As I secured a rope in the maple tree and affixed a swing, I could see Walter watching from his room, a broad smile illuminating his face. Even from the long distance, I could feel the passion in his warm blue eyes.

"Damn, pinch me," I thought.

"You've activated the outside to my children," he said, as I lay my head on his chest, my favorite resting place.

Together, we weeded and planted and watered, excavating treasures that revealed a hidden past. Clearly, there had been children and animals in residence at one time. The soil was soft and long ago tended.

Then, *Boom!* Pandemic.

Plagues are like broken hearts and red station wagons. They have been around forever but you don't notice them until you have one of your very own.

The last time I witnessed my species hugging, dancing, and celebrating ritual was February 29, 2020, a leap year. I was the photographer, cantilevered on a linen-draped table full of candles, the DJ holding my legs to keep me from falling. Tears of joy stung my cheeks as I captured frame after frame of the whirling Horah, dragging my camera's shutter to illustrate the blur. The celebrated child white-knuckled her chair as her family spun her high above the happy dance. Oblivious to what the near future would hold, none of us could begin to conceive the depth of loss, the devastation, disorder, and grief ahead, nor the degree to which we would miss us, as a community, as a nation, as a member of the human race.

The next morning, back in Oakland, my downstairs tenant called a sit-down meeting. Surrounding her at the dining room table were masks, gloves, and antiseptic wipes. An employee of the Food and Drug Administration, she was privy to early information.

"This is going to be bad," she informed us. "Every surface of everything you touch has to be wiped down. We'll need to wash hands every time we enter the house. You should be wearing a mask any time you are outside."

People who wore masks in public had always struck me as impolite. Not seeing a smile or grimace would change the way we communicated.

Two weeks later, Gavin Newsom, California's Governor, declared a state of emergency and required all residents of California to "shelter in place." Coronavirus-19, shortened to COVID-19, was to change our lives forever. This lockdown meant no school, no work, no gatherings, no events, nothing, with the exception of grocery shopping, and that, in itself, was dangerous.

Quite by providence, I had introduced myself to Walt's ex-wife just weeks earlier to let her know that I was becoming involved in her children's lives and that she could trust that I was on her side. I reached out again, and she agreed, yes, if anything, I could be a help in keeping them safe and germ-free. *Phew.*

The drive to the city twice a week was spectacular, as traffic had vanished. I couldn't catch a cold or get a parking ticket to save my life. The streets were completely empty, businesses boarded-up, the skies eerily silent. On the news, we watched the number of deaths surge across the globe. No country, none of our species was unaffected, as hospital beds filled up in every corner.

I had worked arduously to keep Walter at a length he was comfortable with. Clearly an introvert, I was not his first thought when he dropped the kids off with his ex for a week alone. Sometimes he'd call, but it was usually several days into his solitude. I had slipped a few times, asking if he could be more attentive with texts, wishing I could count on him should something happen to me, once even asking him if he and the kids would consider a life in Oakland. With each of these overtures, he would recoil, and I would step back.

Restaurants, salons, theaters, bars, and malls remained shut down as spring began. We wiped everything down with sanitizing wipes, including our steering wheels and door handles. When out of the house, we did our grocery shopping without glasses as the masks made them fog up, like a wet windshield. Then, we'd rush into the house to wash our hands. Toilet paper was impossible to find, as was enough protective wear for health care workers. Our hands grew rough from the hand sanitizers.

In March, I watched, as the number of worldwide deaths catapulted from sixteen thousand to twenty-four thousand within a week. By mid-April, we were at a hundred and fifty thousand, with no end in sight. Yet, Walt and I were in our own crescendo. Gardening, cooking, and games with the kids. We'd each go to our respective homes so I could write, and he could continue his job on architectural projects. We'd become a bit of a team.

"Okay," Melody chimed in as we were painting a bird feeder on the living room floor. "We have a yard, we can't go to school. Daddy is working from the kitchen table. *Umm . . .* "

Days later, Walt twisted his head to one side. He was face down on my bed, in full massage mode. Very good at putting time aside for "caressing," this evening, it was my turn to do the giving. "I don't know," Walt purred, "maybe I do this dog thing."

As we'd neared our two-year-going-steady mark, I made a confession. "I've been viewing porn."

"*Hmmm?*" Walt smiled as he turned over, thinking a front massage would be in order.

"Puppy porn." Climbing off the bed, I put on a flannel shirt and lifted my laptop from the bedside table, then flounced back on the bed, propping myself up with an ample set of pillows.

"Look!" I said, scrolling through the bookmarked web pages. "I'm really just window shopping, but will you look at these babies? I've been courting all of the shelters and breeders just to see what's out there."

Walt's eyes scanned the screens of puppies, his mouth curling up at the sides.

"I was thinking of naming him Walter," I said, fawning over an infantile version of my Rick.

"Let's do it." He rested his head back on folded arms, giving me his "why not?" frown.

I couldn't believe it.

"But we're not going to name him Walter."

For Melody, my birthday present was late by a week. My son, Henry, had accompanied me to the hot central valley to pick up what was to be the last choice of the litter. Supernaturally, the remaining pup was the one I'd wanted, since the pictures had started posting eight weeks earlier. The spitting image of Rick, it was clearly the work of God. I bundled his tiny body in a borrowed cat carrier and presented it to Melody, moments after giving her the gift of his dog tag.

Tucker. She had named him herself when we'd asked her in passing what she might name a dog if that ever were to happen. Completely surprised, it was a golden moment, introducing her to a faithful friend she would have for fifteen years.

Tucker was impossible from the start. Splitting between the two households, he was a bra-stealing, house-pooping terror. Getting larger every day, exercise and training was a full-time job. I must not have remembered doing this before. I felt in the presence of a toddler, entering every room to another nightmare of shredded tissues, disheveled tables, and chewed-up area rugs.

"We're together" was a saying we used to assuage all stress and loss. "That's all that matters."

COVID-19 continued to soar out of control. Globally, by August deaths reached nine hundred thousand, with nearly twenty-five million confirmed cases. I hadn't worked since February, but luckily my mortgage was in forbearance until I could work again. When would that be? All rituals, all gatherings were cancelled until further notice. No one could enter my studio. More buildings were boarding up, the looming Salesforce Tower remained dark. The only people leaving their houses were essential workers—those manning the grocery stores and the heroes, our doctors and nurses. Kim's sweet daughter, Mary, whom I had watched marry under a Midwestern oak tree just a few years earlier, had graduated from nursing school and was immediately put in the COVID-19 ward in Missouri. At age twenty-five, our sweet girl was zipping up at least one body bag per night. The silent killer was oppressive.

Zoom became the new way to work and visit loved ones. We gathered in front of our laptops, joyful to see anyone, hungering to hug, to touch, to smell. These things, however, I could still do with my Walter, as he worked arduously via Zoom. I could set a smoothie in front of him and bury my face in his hair, inhaling his sublime musk, as Tucker destroyed the furniture.

The United States government was likewise frighteningly disheveled. The Black Lives Matter movement was fueled by multiple murders of black men and women by police officers. Our inept and bullying President was making public appearances without a mask. White supremacy and anti-mask groups were heating up to a boil.

I had no work, but I could finish this book. Writing was my catharsis, as I joked that the Goddess warned that if I didn't get my butt in the chair to finish my story, she would shut down the entire globe, which she apparently had. I found a publisher who would allow me my funky title and decided to run a Kickstarter campaign to cover my expenses. Scores, if not a hundred of my friends, expressed interest in supporting me, so I felt comfortable with the ask.

As COVID-19 cases neared fifty million, Alice and I Zoomed a film, using darling Tucker as our alluring mascot. I had thirty days to raise eleven thousand dollars. If my target was not reached, I would receive nothing. I selected the date September 11, 2020, and hit "Launch."

The strategy for marketing was to hit your audience five times. First, social media, then, an email, followed by texts and calls.

"Hoorah!" My friends, clients, and acquaintances responded. "Good for you."

"So, log in and fund me, please. You can buy a book in advance."

"I thought I could, but I really can't right now," so many said.

My self-esteem plummeted as the days passed, my efforts unavailing.

"I was thinking you might be one that would put in a few thousand bucks?" I reminded a wealthy client.

"I was going to," he said, smiling at me over a FaceTime call, "but we've got an election coming up, and I need to put all of my money into the Joe Biden campaign."

"Of course," I whimpered. "Maybe I picked a bad time."

Then, came the California wildfires. Now, with two reasons to wear masks wherever we went, the air quality went from bad to intolerable. September, the month that never failed to greet us with dreamy Indian summers, was devoid of light and oxygen.

Everything was terrifying. The need for funding, the lack of work, the election, the pandemic, the fires, the difficult puppy. I was needing more emotional support than Walt seemed capable of giving me. Out of utter fear, I texted him late one September night:

> You're not here for me! I need you and you're not available for me. Where are you? I can't hang my hat on you. Maybe this going steady thing is not going to work.

That was a mistake. I received an email from Walt the next day that ended our love affair in four short sentences. "I can't give you the attention you need. I'm too busy. You're more attracted to me than I am to you. I'll always love you."

Moments later, my phone signaled an incoming text.

> I have told the children that we have broken up. Let's figure out the puppy.

I was blinded with shock and backpedaling as fast as I could.

> But we have the holidays coming up. We were hoping to bring the kids to Hawaii. We just got a pupy together. This cannot happen. We need to sit down and talk.

> I've moved on.

Where does one move in a pandemic? We were in our private social bubble. He was one of the few people I was allowed to touch.

I was crestfallen. The man who moved all of my planets and pulled all of my strings changed in one day.

On one side of our emotional spectrum lives love. Qualities such as generosity, abundance, forgiveness, and tenderness buoy and empower us, giving us secure scaffolding and joyful hope. When our outlook is love-centered, there is almost nothing we cannot endure or achieve. On the other side, we have fear. Dwelling with fear lives rage, jealousy, racism, loneliness, anxiety, cruelty. I felt fear. I triggered fear in Walt's heart and he was gone overnight.

Why had I done this and how could I fix it? How did he fall out of love without my permission? Walter had proved to be a coward, a complete stranger. Within a week, he was seeing another woman, putting his fear of intimacy before his children. There was only one person in our circle that could understand it . . . his mother.

"It's exactly what his father did. It's proclivity."

The following three months were heavy and grief-filled. Unable to eat or sleep, I paced and wept and paced and wept, chain-smoking, seeking out windy shores to hold me. Reaching in the darkness for my parents, my God, my reason to live. Naturally, it was Kim, long-distance, who held tight to my heart, assuring me daily that this was not my fault.

As 2020 wound down, our beleaguered, divided, Swiss-cheese nation was beyond exhausted. There was nothing left to eat but our own souls. As the death toll soared past two million, there weren't enough freezers to hold all of the dead bodies. Our economy was ravaged, our survival seemed beyond perception. My garden had gone fallow, coyotes had stolen my chickens, my hair was a mass of knots, my chess set was toppled and destroyed by a puppy that I'd wanted to share with the best baby I'd ever had. The loneliness was crippling. Was he not lonely?

In his attempt to get as far from fear as possible, Walter had villainized me to his kids. After several months of handing off a confused animal, I decided it was time to let him go. I met Walter at the park and offered up Tucker, but Walt couldn't or wouldn't hear me. He couldn't even look me in the eye.

"I have to go" was all he could say. "I'm in love with another."

"I guess you're mine now, little fellow." Holding his then-fifty-pound body in my arms, I did the final scroll through the countless images on my phone of our little family COVID-19 pod. I shuffled through the book of photos of baby Tucker nose-to-nose with Melody, the comedic drawings she'd contributed, confidant that our alliance was secured. I'd been confident too, or I'd not have agreed to get a dog together. We'd never once had an argument or altercation.

President Trump, refusing to accept the election results of his defeat, incited an incendiary insurrection on our nation's Capital by a blood thirsty mob of white supremacists, killing five and threatening our sacred democracy within an inch of its well-worked life. The world watched in amazement as a bare-chested man wearing a furry, horned headpiece shouted, "hang Mike Pence!" The President's final blow of betrayal—things really couldn't get worse.

Yet, as all of the inhabitants of the globe cautiously lifted themselves from the wreckage, squinting through the ashes and stars circling our heads from so many blows, what came into focus was a woman. A venerable Goddess of color from our own Oakland, donning a dazzling purple pantsuit.

Joe Biden and Kamala Harris had won the election. Trump had retreated to his gold-plated castle in a defeated huff, stating he would not attend the inauguration. Our Yertle the Turtle had toppled from his throne and landed facedown in the mud. Moderna and Pfizer announced the development of a vaccine for the coronavirus, and millions across the world were standing in lines in stadiums and parking lots to receive the gift of salvation, reminiscent of taking communion. Hope was on the horizon, and the rain of a new year came in with a deluge, cleaning our parched and blistered landscape, bringing triumphant promise.

New pink magnolias began to blush bright in my yard, beckoning me to the garden again as days turned into weeks.

Sitting on the banks of the Bay's rocky coast, my arms around a hound I had wanted to sire with sweet Melody and Jack, I leaned in to smell his deep fur. Tucker tenderly licked my hand, letting it rest on my skin, easing my incapacitating loneliness.

"Good pup." I exhaled long, as we watched hundreds of shorebirds rise, merge, circle, and land in a swarming, glittery formation. "Way to put a bird on that, huh?"

So, now, this is what my older, wiser, neoteric self knows to be true . . .

The mermaids are still in their colonies, brushing and braiding the sweetgrass of Mother Earth, extolling wisdom for our sailors. I listen for the sirens, and lead with the deepest love I can find. I feel comfort in the net of men and women working for a strong unity because the truth is, I am pretty sure . . .

All are needed by each one. Nothing is fair or good alone.

Sure, I'm a strong, independent woman, but from these catastrophes I say, "I don't want to do this alone. I want a partner to talk to, to trust, to share my umbrella."

Will I go back online, once this pandemic is under control? Will I work again, finish the Goddess Project?

No, I will not go back online. I will return to my circles of light, stepping into each one that illuminates my path. I will get back to my garden, embrace my animals, and revel in the miracle of music. My tool of glass will continue to operate, until my last breath, for certain. I will discover myself in dissimilar fellows. Still in the pandemic, I end this piece with ravenous anticipation, looking toward our future.

In the darkest den, love brings relief; love always wins.

I like that.

Acknowledgments

I have the greatest respect for the gifted wordsmiths I've had the privilege to photograph. Their work gave agency to a new way of expressing a satisfying story, beyond one dimension. It was Betsy Graziani Fasbinder who asked if she could support my story, and did so lovingly. Brooke Warner, Peggy Orenstein, and Ali Binazir gave light to important lessons, and Lisa Dailey let me keep my title, working arduously on my project.

The men and women with whom I related live in my fabric forever, along with Alice, of course, my whole reason to discuss love.

Dani and Summer, you know who you are.

A big shout-out to my Kickstarter backers for the financial support.

Last, but not least, special thanks to my oldest friend, Kimberley, for a lifetime of infallible friendship.

About the Author

Reenie is an observer of light and shade in every aspect of her life. Owner/operator of a photography studio in the Oakland Hills, she's been documenting for over twenty years. She created a pictorial coffee-table book for her beloved village in 2013, and is currently working on "The Goddess Project," highlighting women of political change.

Reenie is a Bay Area native and California historian, contributing to several Oakland publications. Her two children and two stepchildren are grown and nearby. She lives in the Oakland Hills with several chickens, cats, and her puppy, Tucker.

Illustrator

Alice always has a fresh loaf of bread in her oven and an army of happy plants in her home. An accomplished yogi, seamstress, botanist, chef, painter, and wine educator, she also regularly travels internationally to learn firsthand about developing countries, and studies how new advancements in Psychology and Sociology interplay with Data Analytics.

Alice is a member of the ACLU, NPR, NCHRA, Unicorn Riot, ActBlue, The Bail Project, Amnesty International, Communities United Against Police Brutality, and Youth for Human Rights. Alice resides in a renovated warehouse in the East Bay that has more square footage allocated for plants than for humans.

CPSIA information can be obtained
at www.ICGtesting.com
Printed in the USA
FSHW011803140621